Globalisation

This book is due for return on or before the last date shown below.

Independence

Educational Publishers

Cambridge

First published by Independence
PO Box 295
Cambridge CB1 3XP
England

British Library Cataloguing in Publication Data
Globalisation – (Issues Series)
I. Donnellan, Craig II. Series
337

ISBN 1 86168 206 9

Printed in Great Britain
The Burlington Press
Cambridge

Typeset by
Claire Boyd

Cover
The illustration on the front cover is by
Pumpkin House.

CONTENTS

Overview

Chapter One: The Debate

Introduction

Globalisation is the fifty-fifth volume in the **Issues** series. The aim of this series is to offer up-to-date information about important issues in our world.

Globalisation looks at the impact of globalisation on world trade.

The information comes from a wide variety of sources and includes:
Government reports and statistics
Newspaper reports and features
Magazine articles and surveys
Literature from lobby groups
and charitable organisations.

It is hoped that, as you read about the many aspects of the issues explored in this book, you will critically evaluate the information presented. It is important that you decide whether you are being presented with facts or opinions. Does the writer give a biased or an unbiased report? If an opinion is being expressed, do you agree with the writer?

Globalisation offers a useful starting-point for those who need convenient access to information about the many issues involved. However, it is only a starting-point. At the back of the book is a list of organisations which you may want to contact for further information.

*****

Globalisation

Information from Save the Children

Globalisation is a short way of describing how people around the world have become much more interconnected. People who geographically live far apart have been brought closer by a kind of revolution in global trading, electronic communications and the faster spread of ideas and culture. There are good and bad sides to this, especially for children.

In the past, people lived in their own close-knit communities without much contact with the one down the road, never mind people from other cultures and countries. Today, that's all changed. Different communities, cultures and countries are all linked up, interacting and depending on each other.

For example, you may buy a football that was made by children in a village in Pakistan. They have to work to earn money for their families, so that you can carry on playing. Your bit of fun may have cost these children a lot, because their need to work means they miss out on school. On the other hand, they don't want you to stop buying footballs, because then they will be out of work and their families will be worse off. They also depend on big multinational companies, that sell sports goods world-wide, to make the link between them and you. That is globalisation in action.

Save the Children does not oppose globalisation in principle. But it has to be for everyone's benefit.

What's good about it?

One argument about globalisation is that it offers people unique opportunities to develop – socially and economically – because it is much easier to trade goods between countries and continents. In theory, the more goods that are exchanged,

Save the Children

the more money is pumped into the economy, which creates more jobs, which should help to cut poverty. When a society gets richer, it can also afford better health care and education for its children, so they benefit directly.

The Internet is another positive aspect of globalisation. It doesn't just generate business, it also allows people to spread campaigning messages around the world, and raise awareness of important issues. The Internet can be very democratic, potentially giving anyone access to millions of other people.

On a more personal note – need help with your homework? Surf the net and find the answers. Want to find new friends? Anyone can create their own web site and beam it around the globe.

And what's bad?

The Internet is only great if you can log on to it. Poorer people don't get a look-in. Children who haven't even got electricity get left further and further behind in the global race. The Internet is meaningless to billions who lack the skills and technology to use it.

The gap between rich and poor children is growing. Though some people are doing nicely, a few global companies control most of the wealth and power, leaving the great majority of people poor outsiders. Half the world's poor are children. At least 600 million children exist on less than 60p a day.

Increasing family poverty and easier cross-border trade exposes children to particular risks. One of the worst examples is commercial sex abuse; traffickers forcing children to become sex workers and 'trading' them like cheap goods across international borders.

The pressure on poor countries to expand their business overseas

means growing more crops for export – like coffee, tobacco and flowers. Land that was once used to grow food for local people is being used to grow 'luxury' crops that will be flown overseas to relatively well-off consumers. For example, most ordinary Kenyan families can't afford those nice green beans you see in supermarkets, labelled 'Produce of Kenya.' They are mostly grown for export to the West.

This emphasis on export crops, which is part of something called structural adjustment, can force small farmers to the wall. Structural adjustment is a set of policies that were meant to shake up poorly performing economies and generate more wealth. These policies were created by the International Monetary Fund (IMF) and the World Bank. The World Bank is a lending bank for poor countries, while the IMF tries to stabilise the world's economy. Many of the world's poorest countries have had to accept these reforms to get more funding. Structural adjustment policies include privatising government businesses, exporting more goods and cutting government spending on public services like health care and education. This involves making many workers redundant, and cutting

or freezing wages. While economic reform is often very necessary, these policies have hurt poor families and deepened their poverty, because the prices of food, medicines, health care and schooling have all increased while parents' incomes have dropped.

So what is the answer?

Globalisation can be a force for good, so long as it doesn't expose children to greater poverty and risks, such as dangerous work. People in power have to be aware of the effects of global economic change on children; all too often, their needs and lives aren't taken into account.

What is Save the Children doing?

We are:

- Talking to big companies and trying to influence them to act responsibly towards children and their families. For example, in Pakistan, we are working with football makers to phase out child labour and make sure that children who have to work also get an education;
- A member of the Ethical Trading Initiative, which aims to improve the working conditions of people who make goods for European markets;

- Campaigning for debt relief for the poorest countries, and fairer terms of global trade;
- Supporting projects that help the most vulnerable victims of structural adjustment – women and children – to cope with economic change. We also try to convince powerful people to adopt policies that won't cause this harm in the first place.

If you want to find out more about Save the Children's work or you wish to get involved, visit www.savethechildren.org.uk or contact Education Unit, Save the Children, 17 Grove Lane, London SE5 8RD. Tel: 020 7703 5400. E-mail: yep@scfuk.org.uk

• The above information is from the IntroSheet on *Globalisation – A* guide to today's issues from Save the Children's youth education programme. The IntroSheets are updated regularly on the Save the Children web site. Visit www.savethechildren.org.uk/rightonline and click on the link 'Need Info?' to view the latest information. Alternatively, for additional information and web site addresses of Save the Children see page 41 of this book.

© Save the Children

What is globalisation . . .

. . . and when did it begin? Information from www.globalisationguide.org

One can be sure that virtually every one of the 2822 academic papers on globalisation written in 1998 included its own definition, as would each of the 589 new books on the subject published in that year.

Many see it as a primarily economic phenomenon, involving the increasing interaction, or integration, of national economic systems through the growth in international trade, investment and capital flows.

However, one can also point to a rapid increase in cross-border social, cultural and technological exchange as part of the phenomenon of globalisation.

The sociologist, Anthony Giddens, defines globalisation as a decoupling of space and time, emphasising that with instantaneous communications, knowledge and culture can be shared around the world simultaneously.

Globalisation is the rapid increase in cross-border economic, social, technological exchange under conditions of capitalism

---

A Dutch academic who maintains a good web site on globalisation, www.globalize.org, Ruud Lubbers, defines it as a process in which geographic distance becomes a factor of diminishing importance in the establishment and maintenance of cross-border economic, political and socio-cultural relations

Left critics of globalisation define the word quite differently, presenting it as worldwide drive toward a globalised economic system dominated by supranational corporate trade and banking institutions that are not accountable to democratic processes or national governments.

Globalisation is an undeniably

capitalist process. It has taken off as a concept in the wake of the collapse of the Soviet Union and of socialism as a viable alternate form of economic organisation.

Try this: Globalisation is the rapid increase in cross-border economic, social, technological exchange under conditions of capitalism.

When did globalisation begin?

There is no agreed starting point, but understanding of globalisation is helped by considering the following.

The first great expansion of European capitalism took place in the sixteenth century, following the first circumnavigation of the earth in 1519 to 1521.

There was a big expansion in world trade and investment in the late nineteenth century. This was brought to a halt by the First World War and the bout of anti-free trade protectionism that led to the Great Depression in 1930. Some see this period as an interruption to the process of globalisation commenced in the late nineteenth century.

A sense that the world was united was generated by the establishment of the International Date Line and world time zones, together with the near global adoption of the Gregorian calendar between 1875 and 1925. During that period, international standards were also agreed for telegraphy and signalling.

The end of the Second World War brought another great expansion of capitalism with the development of multinational companies interested in producing and selling in the domestic markets of nations around the world. The emancipation of colonies created a new world order. Air travel and the development of international communications enhanced the progress of international business.

The fall of the Berlin Wall and the collapse of the Soviet Union ended the cold war between the forces of capitalism and socialism with capitalism triumphant. The development of the internet made possible the organisation of business on a global scale with greater facility than ever before.

An excellent paper exploring this, and other issues relating to globalisation, is written by Mauro Guillen, at the Wharton School and Department of Sociology at the University of Pennsylvania. The paper, *Is Globalization Civilizing, Destructive Or Feeble? A Critique Of Five Key Debates In The Social-Science Literature*, can be downloaded from: knowledge.wharton.upenn.edu/ show_paper.cfm?id=938

• The above information is an extract from: www.globalisationguide.org The Globalisation Guide is designed as a resource for students. It presents the arguments of both those who believe globalisation is a force for good and those who believe it is a force for evil.

© Australian APEC Study Centre

A global glossary for beginners

Crack the code

A beginner's guide to globalisation

We all play a role in the great globalisation game. The best way to make full use of our power as citizens and consumers is by getting a grip of the different terms involved. This global glossary will get you started.

Capitalism

Capitalism is an economic system and ideology based around the idea of people trading on a market, owning private property and accumulating capital to invest in financial or industrial enterprises. Most people in a capitalist system work for private employers, providing goods or services that are sold for profit. The state employs few people, owns no enterprises and puts few regulations on the economy.

Anti-capitalism

Anti-capitalism is a very broad term which shot into the media spotlight during the 1999 WTO summit in Seattle, where a range of people and organisations demonstrated against how the world's international economic system works. The term can cover any challenge to capitalism as the best or only way to organise the world.

Liberalisation

Liberalisation is a process of reducing the government's involvement in a country's economy, based on the idea that private businesses can run things more efficiently. It normally involves de-regulation (removing government regulation and restrictions), privatisation (sale of state-owned enterprises to the private sector) and

opening up economies (removing trade barriers – see Free trade).

Structural adjustment

Structural adjustment is a set of policy changes countries have to make in order to receive loans through the IMF and World Bank. It often involves liberalisation of the economy. Structural adjustment is intended to help countries become more economically efficient so they can easily repay their loans, but it has been strongly criticised for creating unemployment, and making health and education too expensive for many people.

Free trade

Free trade means governments have to treat local and foreign producers the same, for example by not creating barriers against importing goods, services or people from other countries, or giving national businesses and farmers an advantage over foreign firms by offering them financial support. In practice, truly free trade has never existed, and reducing trade barriers is always subject to intense political negotiation between countries of unequal power.

Ethical trade

Ethical trade involves companies finding ways to buy their products from suppliers who provide good working conditions, and respect the environment and human rights.

Fair trade

Fair trade encourages small-scale producers to play a stronger role in managing their relationship with buyers, guaranteeing them a fair financial return for their work.

World Trade Organisation

The World Trade Organisation (WTO) was created in 1994 to liberalise world trade through international agreements. Based in Geneva, the WTO has 140 member countries, some of which have much more power than others. For instance, Japan has 25 delegates while Malawi cannot afford to keep any staff in Geneva.

International Monetary Fund

The International Monetary Fund (IMF) was set up in 1944 along with the World Bank to maintain a stable international trading system. It monitors countries' economies, and gives out loans to help the international economic system function more smoothly. The IMF can impose conditions on countries wishing to borrow money. All borrowers must pay back the loan within a specified time and are charged interest.

World Bank

The World Bank is the main organisation providing financial help for development. Originally established to help Europe recover after the Second World War, it has also provided loans for structural adjustment in developing countries since 1980. By 1990, developing countries owed the World Bank US$89 billion in debt. Smaller regional development banks in Africa, Asia and Latin America work in the same way, but with fewer resources.

The Quad

The Quad is a name given to the four most economically and politically powerful groups of countries in world trade: the European Union, the United States, Japan and Canada. They don't always agree on policy, but when their interests coincide they become a very dominant group in forums like the WTO.

Debt

Debt is money a government owes to either another country, private creditors, or international agencies like the IMF or World Bank.

Aid

Aid means transferring resources from industrial to developing countries in many different ways: one country can support a specific project in another; an international organisation can decide to spend money on supporting a country's economy; specialised staff or equipment can provide technical assistance, or loans are given with a special repayment rate.

Multi-National Corporations

Multi-National Corporations (MNCs) are companies that operate in many different countries beyond the one where they are registered. An MNC sells its products and services globally, and often has offices and staff in several countries. Its products are often made step by step across several continents. The world has a rapidly growing number of MNCs, which are becoming increasingly powerful.

Links

- Go Bananas and Choices, two games exploring international trade issues, are available from Oxfam on 01865 313185.
- Contact the Fairtrade Foundation on www.fairtrade.org.uk or call 020 7405 5942.
- For information about poverty and globalisation, contact the World Development Movement. Freephone 0800 328 2153, e-mail wdm@wdm.org.uk or visit www.wdm.org.uk
- *Global Eye* is a magazine about world development. Call 020 8763 2555, e-mail info@worldaware.org.uk or visit www.globaleye.org.uk
- Find out about British aid from the Department for International Development (DFID) on www.dfid.gov.uk, e-mail enquiry@dfid.government.uk or call 0845 300 410.

• The above information is an extract from *RightAngle*, the magazine produced by Save the Children. For more information see their web site at www.savethechildren.org.uk or see page 41 for their postal address details.

© Save the Children

The World Bank

The World Bank was established to bring prosperity to Europe in the post-war era. Now it is the target of anti-globalisation violence. Philip Pank examines the issues

So what is the World Bank?

The International Bank for Reconstruction and Development, commonly known as the World Bank, is a UN affiliate set up to finance projects that further the economic development of its member nations. Its foundations were laid at the UN monetary and financial conference at Bretton Woods in 1944. It officially came to life in 1946.

What does the bank do?

Back in the post-war era, the bank made loans for the reconstruction of Europe. As the rubble began to be rebuilt, the emphasis shifted from Europe to the developing world. It sought to address an apparent bias against lending money to poor countries. That meant that by the late 1950s, the bank was issuing loans for economic development in Africa, Asia, the Middle East and Latin America.

Where does the money go?

In the fiscal year 2000, the bank lent almost $16bn (£12bn) to its client countries. It says that its dream 'is a world free of poverty' and that it invests money in projects which it thinks will lead developing countries 'onto a path of stable, sustainable and equitable growth'.

Its ethos is simple: countries that are open to international trade, are diversified, attract foreign direct investment and adhere to free market economic policies are the most likely countries to sustain growth. It is a case of capitalism will feed itself. The theory goes that, by encouraging countries to pursue US-style economic management and by attracting private investment, economies will grow and poverty will die as a knock-on effect.

Much of the money, then, goes on efforts to strengthen banks and capital markets, and on projects that aim to create more 'efficient' and

less corrupt public institutions. Another slice of money is loaned for projects in countries where private investors are unwilling to invest in infrastructure such as water supply and sanitation, services which have an overbearing influence on poor people's lives.

Where does the bank get its money?

There are three main sources of funds for the bank: subscriptions paid up by member countries, bond flotation on the world's financial markets and net earnings on the bank's assets.

Who are its members?

There are 183 member countries. All members must first join the International Monetary Fund. Members are shareholders in the bank. They do not all pull equal weight within the organisation. The leading contributors, and therefore those with the biggest say in World Bank policy, are: the United States, Japan, Germany, France and the United Kingdom. Each of these five countries has a nominee on the bank's board of executive directors. The remaining 178 countries are between them allowed to nominate a total of 19 other board members. It is this select board that decides on the bank's work.

The institution is adamant that it remains vital to ensure that the poorest countries can benefit from globalisation

---

So the rich and powerful decide where the money goes?

That should come as no surprise, even to the most die-hard anti-capitalist protester. Some more moderate critics argue that while it is normal for the richest countries to choose who they are willing to help, the methods used are too narrowly focused. The critics say that to invest in projects that seek to smash corruption, for example, will do little to alleviate long-term poverty unless and until the entire international economic system is reformed and made fairer.

But isn't some help better than none?

Again, the critics say not. They argue that the loans given to developing nations have simply made them even poorer. Interest payments on loans suck up money which could go to feed the poor.

And the critics say that the bank attaches far too many strings to its loans. For example, in return for debt relief Benin, the poverty-stricken African country, was forced to liberalise its cotton sector and introduce a performance-based pay structure for civil servants. Zambia was forced to privatise its copper mines in return for relief. The move led to 60,000 job losses in the sector.

Do the problems mean the bank is dead?

Its overhaul from an institution created to salvage war-torn Europe to the guarantor of prosperity the world over has been fraught with problems. The bank admits in its last report that 'the task ahead is daunting'.

However, the institution is adamant that it remains vital to ensure that the poorest countries can benefit from globalisation. It believes it is the right body to find ways of ensuring that debt relief eases poverty and of giving people opportunity rather than charity.

The IMF

The IMF was established to promote international financial stability, but critics claim it has contributed to global inequality

What is the IMF and what does it do?

The International Monetary Fund is a UN agency set up by the 1944 Bretton Woods conference to secure financial stability in the world economy.

How does it work?

It seeks to promote international monetary cooperation, exchange stability, and orderly exchange arrangements in its 183 member states. Hard currency is also lent to countries experiencing balance of payments deficits, probably the most important part of its work.

What makes the IMF unpopular?

It is the economic reforms it insists upon as conditions for financial assistance. Critics say that since the 1980s the IMF has abandoned its original mission in favour of restructuring national economies along a US model once favoured by Ronald Reagan. Restructuring plans (now named 'poverty reduction strategies') list an average of 114 conditions per country in return for capital. In each case, those on the receiving end have to remove trade barriers, sell national assets to foreign investors, slash social spending and crush trade unions.

By Simon Jeffery

Who is affected?

Largely third world and developing countries. For example, Tanzania was forced to charge for hospital visits and school fees. Hospital treatment fell by 53% and the illiteracy rate soared. In Ecuador, the IMF ordered 26,000 job cuts along with a halving of real wages for the remaining workers. Meanwhile, it demanded the sale of the water system to foreign owners and an 80% increase in the price of cooking oil.

What is it thinking?

The IMF is dominated by neo-liberal economics that decree countries are best served by making an easy fit

At present, the rich nations are becoming richer and the developing world, crippled by debt repayment and 'restructuring', has little control over its economic future

with the world economy. Globalisation allows them to provide products and services demanded by external markets and – the theory goes – bring in foreign investment. The removal of trade barriers and employment legislation makes the newly restructured countries more attractive to the multinationals.

Does it work?

GDP and life expectancy did rise in the last 50 years of the twentieth century, but global inequality is growing and – besides – some of these improvements took place in the days before the neo-liberal IMF, when per capita income grew by 74% in South America. At present, the rich nations are becoming richer and the developing world, crippled by debt repayment and 'restructuring', has little control over its economic future – much having already been surrendered.

But we do not know what would have happened to the developing world if the IMF had not given its assistance. The restructuring was – after all – offered at times of economic crisis when previous models were judged to have failed, hit by rising oil costs and instability on the world financial markets.

© Guardian Newspapers Limited 2001

Britain turning against globalisation

British people are suspicious of globalisation – and sympathetic towards the anti-globalisation protesters of Seattle and Genoa – according to surprise new research findings

A new MORI survey, commissioned to coincide with the publication of Anita Roddick's new globalisation book *Take It Personally*, shows that the majority of British people are not convinced about the benefits of globalisation.

The research will come as a shock to Blair and business commentators who have led the assault on the protesters. It also looks set to confirm a growing sense that unrestricted global business is damaging what Britons care about the most – the well-being of their families and communities.

Even three in five Conservative voters reject the accusation that anti-globalisation protesters are simply thugs and anarchists. The research also found that:

The public do not think globalisation is a force for good.
- Only one in eight people bought the official view that globalisation enhances everyone's quality of life (13%).
- As many as 92% believe that multinational companies should meet the highest human health, animal welfare and environment standards wherever they are operating.
- 58% of the public think that 'what's good for business is not good for most people in developing, poorer countries' – and as many as 71% of broadsheet readers reject the idea that global business is good for most people in developing, poorer countries.
- As many as 38% of people believe globalisation actually damages the environment.

The public think the government should stand up to multinationals.
- Between 87% and 92% of people think that the government should protect the environment, employment conditions and health – even when it conflicts with the interests of multi-nationals.

The media are not reflecting mainstream views on globalisation.
From a list of six positive and negative statements about the anti-globalisation protestors the two statements which prompted the strongest agreement were that:
- The protestors were raising genuine concerns and issues shared by many people around the world (41% agreed).
- The media focus on a small number of troublemakers, ignoring the peaceful majority of protestors (38% agreed).

MORI Chairman Professor Robert Worcester described the survey as 'a timely indicator of people's underlying distrust of big companies when it comes to acting in the public interest. The fact that

---

'People aren't stupid. This survey shows that ordinary people are well aware of the negative impacts of globalisation – for themselves, for poor countries, for the environment.'

---

four in ten (41%) of the British public (representing around 18.5 million people) believe the anti-globalisation protestors have a point should prompt a serious rethinking of the globalisation debate.'

Anita Roddick, OBE, said: 'People aren't stupid. This survey shows that ordinary people are well aware of the negative impacts of globalisation – for themselves, for poor countries, for the environment. The public is taking global issues personally; the government and big business would be advised to listen to them.'

This survey was commissioned by Anita Roddick, alongside Thorsons Publishers and communications agency the Forster Company.

Notes:
- Anita Roddick is Founder and Co-Chair of The Body Shop International plc. Thorsons is a division of Harper Collins. The Forster Company is a public interest communications company specialising in environmental and social issues
- The MORI survey was carried out between 20-25 September 2001 among a representative sample of 2,013 members of the British public aged 15+. Data were weighted to reflect the national profile.
- *Take It Personally: How Globalisation affects you and powerful ways to challenge it* is available from Monday 15 October 2001 from all good bookshops.

© MORI

What's wrong with corporations?

Some things you'd probably prefer weren't true about corporations

Corporations aren't allowed to be nice

Company directors are legally obliged to act in the best interests of their shareholders' investments i.e. to make them as much money as possible. Genuine efforts to sacrifice profits in favour of human rights and environmental protection are off-limits. Even if a company's directors took the long view that environmental sustainability is ultimately essential for economic sustainability, their share price would drop and they would probably be swallowed up by competitors. This is why corporate social and environmental initiatives can't really get beyond the marketing and greenwash stage.

Corporations are people too

They may not have human feelings, they may be bloodless and soulless, but in the eyes of the law they are 'persons' with many of the same rights as flesh-and-blood humans. Corporations can claim, for example, the right to freedom of speech, the right to sue, the right to 'enjoyment of possessions' (problematic in planning and environment law). They even have a number of advantages over ordinary people – specifically, corporations can be in two or more places at once (so cannot be jailed) and can divide themselves to dodge liability for their crimes. It is normal, for example, to transfer ownership of a dangerous cargo to a distant subsidiary while the cargo is at sea, so the parent company is not liable if it causes a toxic spill. Also, corporations are ruthless in claiming their rights – after all, they can afford the best lawyers.

Corporations are benefit scroungers

In 1997, British Aerospace (BAe) demanded £120m from the UK government to build a new jet. If the money were not forthcoming, BAe would fund the project itself – abroad. In 1998 the government paid up, and in March 2000 handed over a further £530m for another model. This is routine corporate behaviour. If individuals did it, it would be called blackmail. On the other end of the equation, corporations pay less and less tax. It is estimated that Rupert Murdoch's media empire in the UK paid no net corporation tax in the twelve years to 1999. This means they're living off the services paid for by everyone else – they rely on publicly funded roads to move goods and staff, on the police to protect them from crime, on the NHS to treat sick workers and the education system to train new ones. But these essential services are paid for predominantly by individuals and small businesses.

Corporations are persistent offenders

In the UK, commercial corporations emerged in the 17th century, as a direct result of merchant groups breaking the laws banning corporations from making a profit. From 1825 a few legal companies were set up – initially restricted to building canals and waterworks. After 1844 companies could be established to engage in any business activity stated in their constitution. Even this wasn't enough – up until 1965 corporations consistently broke the law by engaging in other activities not in their articles. In 1965 this law was repealed. On a day-to-day level, this 'battle to free corporations' continues; in tax and labour law, health and safety and environmental protection corporations consistently

break the rules then lobby government, often successfully, to say the rule shouldn't have been there in the first place. Imagine if ordinary criminals had such opportunities . . .

Corporations are as rich as countries
In 1999, according to the Institute for Policy Studies, 51 of the world's 100 largest economies were corporations. To put this in perspective, General Motors is now bigger than Denmark and three-and-a-half times the size of New Zealand; the top 200 corporations' combined sales are bigger than the combined economies of all countries minus the biggest 10. Is it any surprise that they are able to dictate terms to many countries? National governments are often of a dubious moral character, but corporations are by their nature (see above) greedy, inhumane and parasitic, as well as lacking even a veneer of democratic control. Moreover, they share a common hatred of people interfering with their profits and 'rights'. This means they lobby to the same ends and can have massive effects – just look at the current US government.

General Motors is now bigger than Denmark and three-and-a-half times the size of New Zealand

---

But what does all this mean?
Corporations would like us to believe that they are the pinnacle of economic evolution and we should get down on our knees and thank them for condescending to sell us their products. But despite their power, which can sometimes seem overwhelming, corporations are scared to the point of paranoia. Like totalitarian governments, they feel the need to control the theory as well as the practice of our society – the corporate-dominated mainstream media is roped in to reassure us that corporate capitalism is 'like the weather – and you can't change the weather' [from Channel 4 News – after Mayday 2001], there is no alternative, and the place of the people in a democracy is to choose which corporate puppet clone to vote

for once in five years, then go home and consume in peace.

What can we do about it?
Corporations need to be first tamed, then dismantled and replaced by structures people can control. In order to do this we need to understand how they work, to recognise their real motivations and methods, to unpick the captivating rainbow veils spun by advertising and PR and to document the abuses of humanity and nature that occur at each point of the corporations' activities. Corporate Watch does not subscribe to any rigid ideology – we do not claim to be Marxists or anarchists or socialists. Our core belief is simply that society should be run in the best long-term interest of all human beings and other species – not for the short-term gain of transnational corporations. This article relates to the UK, but the situation is similar in most other industrialised countries.

• The above information is an extract from the web site www.corporatewatch.org.uk

Corporate globalisation

Information from CorpWatch

Global reach
- Fifty-one of the world's top 100 economies are corporations.
- Royal Dutch Shell's revenues are greater than Venezuela's Gross Domestic Product. Using this measurement, WalMart is bigger than Indonesia. General Motors is roughly the same size as Ireland, New Zealand and Hungary combined.
- There are 63,000 transnational corporations worldwide, with 690,000 foreign affiliates.
- Three-quarters of all transnational corporations are based in North America, Western Europe and Japan.
- Ninety-nine of the 100 largest transnational corporations are from the industrialised countries.

WTO and global trade: who benefits?
- Since it was created in 1995, the WTO has ruled that every environmental policy it has reviewed is an illegal trade barrier that must be eliminated or changed. With one exception, the WTO also has ruled against every health or food safety law it has reviewed.
- Nations whose laws were declared

Ninety-nine of the 100 largest transnational corporations are from the industrialised countries

---

trade barriers by the WTO – or that were merely threatened with WTO action – have eliminated or watered down their policies to meet WTO requirements.
- Supposedly each of the WTO's 134 member countries has an equal say in governance. In practice, decision-making is dominated by the 'Quad': USA; European Union; Japan and Canada.
- Each member of the Quad represents its corporations' interests at the WTO. These corporations are often directly involved in writing and shaping WTO rules. In the US this is achieved through official 'Trade Advisory Committees' which are dominated by the private sector.

- For instance, the US International Trade Administration's Energy Advisory Committee is made up exclusively of representatives of giant oil, mining, gas and utility corporations, including Texaco, Enron, Halliburton and Freeport-McMoran.
- The top fifth of the world's people in the richest countries enjoy 82% of the expanding export trade and 68% of foreign investment – the bottom fifth, receive roughly 1%.
- Women comprise 70 per cent of the world's 1.3 billion absolute poor. Worldwide, they bear the brunt of economic and financial transition and crisis caused by market forces and globalisation.

NAFTA & FTAA: who benefits?

- Seventy-five per cent of Mexico's population lives in poverty today, compared with 49 per cent in 1981, before Mexico underwent reforms that paved the way for NAFTA – the North American Free Trade Agreement.
- The number of Mexicans living in severe poverty (living on less than $2 a day) has grown by four million since NAFTA began in 1994.
- NAFTA has generated booming industrial development but little investment in the environment. As a result, environmental pollution and related public health problems have increased on both sides of the US-Mexico border.
- In the first four years of NAFTA, 15 wood product companies, including International Paper and Boisie Cascade, set up shop in Mexico, cutting some of North America's largest intact forests.
- Hundreds of thousands of US jobs have shifted to Mexico under NAFTA. 260,000 US workers have qualified for a special NAFTA retraining programme. Especially hard hit are the apparel and electronics industries, major employers of women and people of colour.
- The Free Trade Area of the Americas (FTAA), currently being negotiated by 34 countries, is intended by its architects to be the most far-reaching trade agreement in history.

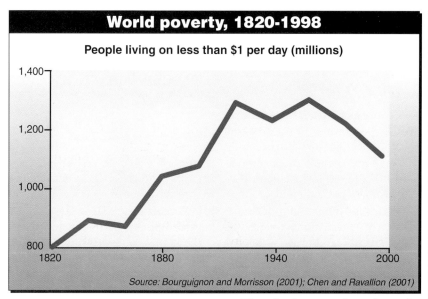

World poverty, 1820-1998
People living on less than $1 per day (millions)

Source: Bourguignon and Morrisson (2001); Chen and Ravallion (2001)

The absolute number of people living in poverty rose in the 1990s in Eastern Europe, South Asia, Latin America and the Caribbean, and sub-Saharan Africa

- Although it is based on the model of NAFTA, the FTAA goes far beyond it in scope and power, potentially granting unequalled new rights to corporations to compete for and even challenge publicly funded government services, including health care, education, social security, culture and environmental protection.

The World Bank and IMF: who benefits?

- In the 1980s and early 1990s, the International Monetary Fund imposed structural adjustment programmes on more than 70 countries.
- Structural adjustment policies have required 36 countries in sub-Saharan Africa – where more than half of the population lives in absolute poverty – to decrease domestic consumption and shift scarce resources into production of cash crops for export; state-owned companies and many state services have been privatised, and health and education expenditures have been cut and restructured.

- The absolute number of people living in poverty rose in the 1990s in Eastern Europe, South Asia, Latin America and the Caribbean, and sub-Saharan Africa – all areas that came under the sway of adjustment programmes.
- Structural adjustment policies have elicited massive protests in countries as far flung as Ecuador, Zambia, the Philippines and Jamaica.
- In 2000 a bipartisan Congressional panel – the Meltzer Commission – found that World Bank Group and IMF failures can be traced to 'overlapping missions, ineffectiveness, corruption, and waste of resources, and failure to develop successful regional programs in agriculture, forestry, environment and health care,' among other problems.
- Each year, the World Bank awards some 40,000 contracts to private firms.
- US Treasury Department calculates that for every US$1 the US contributes to international development banks, US corporations receive more than double that amount in bank-financed procurement contracts.
- The World Bank has an astounding 65-70 per cent failure rate of its projects in the poorest countries.

- The above information is from CorpWatch's web site which can be found at www.corpwatch.org
© CorpWatch

Dump those prejudices

The left must learn to love the World Trade Organisation

Many on the left obsessively loathe the World Trade Organisation, in the way Tory Europhobes hate the European Union. Just as Brussels-bashers peddle lies about the EU, so Naomi Klein, Noreena Hertz and others slander the WTO. That is a pity. The left has warmed to the EU. Now it should reconsider its opposition to the WTO. Believe it or not, the WTO is not against social democracy.

The worst charges against the WTO are these four. First, that it does the bidding of big global companies. Second, that it undermines workers' rights and environmental protection by encouraging a 'race to the bottom' between governments competing for jobs and foreign investment. Third, that it harms the poor. And last, that it is destroying democracy by secretly and unaccountably imposing its writ on the world.

Undeniably, some companies have undue influence over governments. More should be done to separate money and politics. But companies are constrained by competition and regulation – both of which the WTO bolsters. Freeing trade curbs domestic giants by exposing them to foreign competition.

Take BT. For international phone calls, where there is competition, it is just one provider among many. For local calls, where there isn't, it can hold customers and the government to ransom, most recently by delaying the roll-out of broadband internet. The only reason companies like Shell heed protests is that they face competition: if Shell had a monopoly, it could safely have ignored Greenpeace's Brent Spar campaign.

Competition is not a cure-all. Often, governments need to regulate too. And they can. It is a terrible irony that the left has lost faith in government. Governments are not

By Philippe Legrain

impotent. The WTO itself is merely governments acting together to regulate global markets. Brussels has just blocked General Electric, the world's biggest company, from taking over Honeywell. Labour has imposed the utility windfall tax, introduced the minimum wage and ramped up petrol duty.

> *Poverty is terrible. But globalisation can help. While GDP per person fell by 1% a year in the 1990s in non-globalising developing countries, it rose by 5% a year in globalising ones*

So much for the race to the bottom. As the fuel protests showed, the main constraint on government is public opinion, not globalisation or corporate power.

If globalisation is forcing governments to slim down, how come the average tax take in rich OECD countries has risen from 35% to 38% of GDP since 1985? Corporate taxes are a bigger share of government revenues than 20 years ago. Surveys show that skilled workers, good

infrastructure and nearby customers determine where companies invest far more than low taxes and regulation.

Labour and environmental standards are generally rising, not falling. An OECD study found that workers' union rights had not got significantly worse in any of 75 countries since the early 1980s. In 17 (including Brazil, South Korea and Turkey) they had markedly improved. The same study found that pollution havens are a myth. If anything, competition is bidding up environmental standards.

Developing countries are attracting investment not by lowering their standards, but because they are making the best of their comparative advantage. This does not spell doom for British workers. Provided people are equipped with skills to find another job and are protected by a decent welfare system, we can all gain from globalisation. It makes no sense to protect yesterday's jobs at the expense of tomorrow's.

Nor is it fair. How else are the poor going to get richer? It is a funny kind of socialism that stops at national borders. Surely international solidarity means buying t-shirts from Bangladesh as well as demonstrating for debt relief. The fact that seamstresses in Bangladesh are paid less than in Britain does not necessarily mean they are exploited. They earn more than they would as farmers. And however awful conditions in a Nike factory may be, they are usually worse in a local sweatshop.

Poverty is terrible. But globalisation can help. While GDP per person fell by 1% a year in the 1990s in non-globalising developing countries, it rose by 5% a year in globalising ones. The WTO is a friend of the poor. Its rules protect the weak in a world of unequal power. Unlike the United Nations, WTO rules apply to everyone – even the United States. Costa Rica challenged US restrictions on its underwear exports at the

11

WTO – and won. Of course, the WTO is not perfect. But it is better than the law of the jungle, where might equals right.

The worries about democracy are more well-founded. Democracy remains rooted in local communities and nation states. So it is difficult to work together internationally – on global warming or trade, at the EU or the WTO – without leaving voters feeling out of touch. But abolishing the WTO is not a solution. As we learned from the 1930s, beggar-thy-neighbour policies end up making beggars of us all. Nor are world elections to a world parliament and a world government realistic. Sixty million Britons would not accept 1,300m Chinese outvoting them. So the best option is to reform the WTO.

It is already more democratic than you think. All agreements are reached by consensus. Every country has a veto – unlike at the UN, where only big powers do – and WTO agreements are ratified by parliament. The organisation is held to account mainly through government, but also through contacts with MPs, trade unions, business and NGOs, through the media, and through its web site – on which most working documents appear rapidly.

Even so, the WTO should be more open. Government should develop better procedures for informing MPs and voters about its work at the WTO and MPs could hold public hearings to reconnect the WTO with voters. If you hate capitalism, you will probably never support the WTO (although Fidel Castro does). But if, like most people, you believe in markets tempered by government intervention, you should think again about the WTO.

• Philippe Legrain was until recently special adviser to the director-general of the World Trade Organisation

Bridging the global divide

Anti-globalisation cannot help the developing world. But the rich countries must ditch the hypocrisy and keep their promises to the South

The World Trade Organisation (WTO) is meeting again, this time in the unlikely setting of the Gulf state of Qatar. But Doha will not take its place alongside Seattle, Prague, Quebec and Genoa on what seemed to be the 'anti-globalisation world tour' of 1999 to 2001.

The current meeting is taking place without the mass protests, anarchist violence or frenzied media attention of those earlier summits, due to both the remoteness of the Gulf desert venue and the change in the international political climate after September 11th. Very few if any protestors have made it through the massive security cordon erected around the remote desert venue; most of the NGOs present at the demonstrations in Genoa were determined to avoid association with any possible terrorist threat to the Doha meeting.

But the very fact that there has not been a stand-off confrontation provides an important political opportunity. In concert with its European partners the British Government can use this meeting to shift its public stance on the question of 'globalisation'. And the NGOs, who have done much to set a new agenda of global justice and

By Michael Jacobs

legitimacy, must now break with the rhetoric of 'anti-globalisation', focusing attention instead on a constructive agenda for 'global justice'.

Globalisation has become the catchword of the age; but the debate about it has been sunk in confusion

The desired outcome for both should not be another failure like that of Seattle, but agreement that the overwhelming priority of any new trade round must be to reduce poverty in the developing countries of the South.

Globalisation has become the catchword of the age; but the debate about it has been sunk in confusion. Both intellectually and politically it needs recasting.

Intellectually, we have first to escape from the misleading polarity between globalisation and something

called 'anti-globalisation'. The processes by which formerly national forces and trends become global are occurring in several different planes: communications, finance, investment and trade, culture, politics. To be 'against' these processes is not simply futile, because they are not in anyone's power to stop; it is mostly reactionary.

To 'oppose' globalisation is to deny people in poorer countries the benefits of knowledge, technological advance, cultural diversity, travel and international contact which we in the rich world enjoy. There is a genuine anti-globalisation position: it is held by Islamic and other religious fundamentalists who want to turn back the tide of modernity. But no one in progressive politics should be on their side.

Of course, most so-called anti-globalisers acknowledge this. Pressed, they will then redefine their position, saying that what they are really opposed to is not globalisation per se but the neoliberal free trade agenda which (they argue) is its economic and cultural driver. The institutions of the World Trade Organisation, the IMF and the World Bank are cast as the great trinity of villainhood here.

But this too is wrong. Not because free trade is a good thing, but because free trade isn't how the world (or any of these institutions) is organised. The anti-globalisers have been fooled by the rhetoric of their opponents.

Multinational corporations, finance capitalists and Northern governments justify themselves in terms of free trade, but what they actually promote are their own interests, which is not the same thing at all. In trade the industrialised world imposes liberalisation on developing countries while protecting its own markets in agriculture and textiles through tariff barriers. IMF aid conditions force Southern countries to abolish food subsidies – while the EU dumps its own subsidised food surpluses on their markets, crushing local farmers. The IMF forces Southern countries to deregulate their capital markets, while crisis-struck banks and hedge funds in the US are bailed out with billions of dollars.

Exploitative, hypocritical and unjust this is, as the anti-globalisers rightly argue; free trade it isn't.

The social movements now organised against these processes have a critical role to play: they have already forced their concerns onto the agenda of Northern governments and even, in part, the multinationals. But they must escape from the blind alley of 'anti-globalisation' and opposition to the WTO. They must seek, not a reduction in trade or the free-for-all (benefiting only the powerful) that would follow the failure of the WTO, but a new system of trade and investment rules designed to prioritise poverty reduction.

And here they need to make common cause with the social democratic and centre-left governments of Europe, including our own. It is inevitable that demonstrators and governments will find themselves on opposite sides of the barricades: that is in the nature of protest. But the gulf between the two sides exhibited in the bloody scenes at Genoa this summer was deeply depressing. On one side Tony Blair, Jack Straw and Clare Short appeared to show almost no understanding of the reasons why hundreds

of thousands of peaceful protestors, including highly respected NGOs, had taken to the streets. On the other we had the absurdity of George Monbiot, *Guardian* columnist and leading 'anti-globalisation' campaigner, writing that the governments of the G8 were the last people the demonstrators should be seeking to cancel third world debt, since it was they who had created it. But who else does he think can do so? The protestors themselves?

To 'oppose' globalisation is to deny people in poorer countries the benefits of knowledge, technological advance, cultural diversity and travel which we in the rich world enjoy

---

In truth there is much more common cause between most of the 'anti-globalisation' movement and left-of-centre European governments than the rhetoric on both sides would have us believe. The British NGOs, such as Oxfam, the World Development Movement and Friends of the Earth, are now making clear that they support the principle of a multilateral, rules-based trading system: they no longer attack the WTO as an institution in itself.

In the last two years the logic of protest has left the NGOs allied to anti-capitalist and anti-trade groupings such as Globalise Resistance and the Green Party. But this link should now be broken. It is notable that the major NGOs are now speaking about the 'global justice' and 'trade justice' movements rather than 'anti-globalisation'; their separation from the simplistic anti-capitalists now needs to be made explicit. In terms of membership, the NGO wing of the movement is much larger.

In turn the Government needs to offer a new, much more sympathetic rhetoric towards their cause – and to back this up with genuine shifts of position on trade reform at the WTO. In his Party Conference speech, Tony Blair set out an internationalist agenda so that 'out of the shadow of this evil should emerge lasting good', pledging himself to 'justice and prosperity for the poor and dispossessed'. He pointedly referred to the need to open up European markets, 'so that we practise the free trade we are so fond of preaching'. This will be difficult to achieve: the otherwise Socialist French Government is still blocking EU agricultural reform, protecting French farming interests. But in other key areas such as reductions in Northern trade barriers, patent protection of drugs, investment, and trade in services, European governments can support Third World and NGO demands for fairer trade rules. Most of all, they can and must insist that before any new trade round is agreed, Northern governments must keep the promises on access to markets and reduced agricultural subsidies they made in the last round.

Tomorrow, Tony Blair will make a major Mansion House speech on the current international situation. He is expected again to address the question of globalisation. His remarks – but even more the actions of the Western negotiators at the WTO meeting – will show whether the new desire for global justice is just rhetoric on the part of the rich world – or whether we really mean it.

• Michael Jacobs is General Secretary of the Fabian Society
© *Guardian Newspapers Limited 2001*

Assessing globalisation

Information from the World Bank

What is globalisation?

Globalisation is one of the most charged issues of the day. It is everywhere in public discourse – in TV sound bites and slogans on placards, in web sites and learned journals, in parliaments, corporate boardrooms and labour meeting halls. Extreme opponents charge it with impoverishing the world's poor, enriching the rich and devastating the environment, while fervent supporters see it as a high-speed elevator to universal peace and prosperity. What is one to think?

Amazingly for so widely used a term, there does not appear to be any precise, widely-agreed definition. Indeed the breadth of meanings attached to it seems to be increasing rather than narrowing over time, taking on cultural, political and other connotations in addition to the economic. However, the most common or core sense of economic globalisation – the aspect this article concentrates on – surely refers to the observation that in recent years a quickly rising share of economic activity in the world seems to be taking place between people who live in different countries (rather than in the same country). This growth in cross-border economic activities takes various forms:

International trade

A growing share of spending on goods and services is devoted to imports from other countries. And a growing share of what countries produce is sold to foreigners as exports. Among rich or developed countries the share of international trade in total output (exports plus imports of goods relative to GDP) rose from 27 to 39 per cent between 1987 and 1997. For developing countries it rose from 10 to 17 per cent. (The source for many of these data is the World Bank's World Development Indicators 2000.)

Foreign direct investment (FDI)

Firms based in one country increasingly make investments to establish and run business operations in other countries. US firms invested $133 billion abroad in 1998, while foreign firms invested $193 billion in the US. Overall world FDI flows more than tripled between 1988 and 1998, from $192 billion to $610 billion, and the share of FDI to GDP is generally rising in both developed and developing countries. Developing countries received about a quarter of world FDI inflows in 1988-98 on average, though the share fluctuated quite a bit from year to year. This is now the largest form of private capital inflow to developing countries.

Capital market flows

In many countries (especially in the developed world) savers increasingly diversify their portfolios to include foreign financial assets (foreign bonds, equities, loans), while borrowers increasingly turn to foreign sources of funds, along with domestic ones. While flows of this kind to developing countries also rose sharply in the 1990s, they have been much more volatile than either trade or FDI flows, and have also been restricted to a narrower range of 'emerging market' countries.

Overall observations about globalisation

First, it is crucial in discussing globalisation to carefully distinguish between its different forms. International trade, foreign direct investment (FDI), and capital market flows raise distinct issues and have distinct consequences: potential benefits on the one hand, and costs or risks on the other, calling for different assessments and policy responses. The World Bank generally favours greater openness to trade and FDI because the evidence suggests that the pay-offs for economic development and poverty reduction tend to be large relative to potential costs or risks (while also paying attention to specific policies to mitigate or alleviate these costs and risks).

It is more cautious about liberalisation of other financial or capital market flows, whose high volatility can sometimes foster boom-and-bust cycles and financial crises with large economic costs, as in the emerging-market crises in East Asia and elsewhere in 1997-98. Here the emphasis needs to be more on building up supportive domestic institutions and policies that reduce the risks of financial crisis before undertaking an orderly and carefully sequenced capital account opening.

Second, the extent to which different countries participate in globalisation is also far from uniform. For many of the poorest least-developed countries the problem is not that they are being impoverished by globalisation, but that they are in danger of being largely excluded from it. The minuscule 0.4 per cent share of these countries in world trade in 1997 was down by half from 1980. Their access to foreign private investment remains negligible. Far from condemning these countries to continued isolation and poverty, the urgent task of the international community is to help them become better integrated in the world economy, providing assistance to help them build up needed supporting institutions and policies, as well as by continuing to enhance their access to world markets.

Third, it is important to recognise that economic globalisation is not a wholly new trend. Indeed, at a basic level, it has been an aspect of the human story from earliest times, as widely scattered populations gradually became involved in more extensive and complicated economic relations. In the modern era, globalisation saw an earlier flowering towards the end of the 19th century, mainly among the countries that are today developed or rich. For many of these countries trade and capital market flows relative to GDP were close to or higher than in recent years. That earlier peak of globalisation was reversed in the first half of the 20th century, a time of growing protectionism, in a context of bitter national and great-power strife, world wars, revolutions, rising authoritarian ideologies, and massive economic and political instability.

In the last 50 years the tide has flowed towards greater globalisation once more. International relations have been more tranquil (at least compared to the previous half-century), supported by the creation and consolidation of the United Nations system as a means of peacefully resolving political differences between states, and of institutions like the GATT (today the WTO), which provide a framework of rules for countries to manage their commercial policies. The end of colonialism brought scores of independent new actors onto the world scene, while also removing a shameful stain associated with the earlier 19th-century episode of globalisation. The 1994 Uruguay Round of the GATT saw developing countries become engaged on a wide range of multilateral international trade issues for the first time.

The pace of international economic integration accelerated in the 1980s and 1990s, as governments everywhere reduced policy barriers that hampered international trade and investment. Opening to the outside world has been part of a more general shift towards greater reliance on markets and private enterprise, especially as many developing and communist countries came to see that high levels of government planning and intervention were failing to deliver the desired development outcomes.

China's sweeping economic reforms since the end of the 1970s, the peaceful dissolution of communism in the Soviet bloc at the end of the 1980s, and the taking root and steady growth of market-based reforms in democratic India in the 1990s are among the most striking examples of this trend. Globalisation has also been fostered by technological progress, which is reducing the costs of transportation and communications between countries. Dramatic falls in the cost of telecommunications, of processing, storing and transmitting information, make it much easier to track down and close on business opportunities around the world, to coordinate operations in far-flung locations, or to trade online services that previously were not internationally tradable at all.

Finally, given this backdrop, it may not be surprising (though it is not very helpful) that 'globalisation' is sometimes used in a much broader economic sense, as another name for capitalism or the market economy. When used in this sense the concerns expressed are really about key features of the market economy, such as production by privately-owned and profit-motivated corporations, frequent reshuffling of resources according to changes in supply and demand, and unpredictable and rapid technological change. It is certainly important to analyse the strengths and weaknesses of the market economy as such, and to better understand the institutions and policies needed to make it work most effectively. And societies need to think hard about how to best manage the implications of rapid technological change. But there is little to be gained by confusing these distinct (though related) issues with economic globalisation in its core sense, that is the expansion of cross-border economic ties.

Conclusion

The best way to deal with the changes being brought about by the international integration of markets for goods, services and capital is to be open and honest about them. Globalisation brings opportunities, but it also brings risks. While exploiting the opportunities for higher economic growth and better living standards that more openness brings, policy-makers – international, national and local – also face the challenge of mitigating the risks for the poor, vulnerable and marginalised, and of increasing equity and inclusion.

Even when poverty is falling overall, there can be regional or sectoral increases about which society needs to be concerned. Over the last century the forces of globalisation have been among those that have contributed to a huge improvement in human welfare, including raising countless millions out of poverty. Going forward, these forces have the potential to continue bringing great benefits to the poor, but how strongly they do so will also continue to depend crucially on factors such as the quality of overall macroeconomic policies, the workings of institutions, both formal and informal, the existing structure of assets, and the available resources, among many others. In order to arrive at fair and workable approaches to

Over the last century the forces of globalisation have been among those that have contributed to a huge improvement in human welfare

these very real human needs, government must listen to the voices of all its citizens.

References
Dollar, David and Aart Kraay. (2000). *Growth is Good for the Poor.* World Bank.
Edwards, Sebastian. (1998) Openness, Productivity and Growth: What Do We Really Know? *The Economic Journal.* March 1998.
Rodrik, Dani. (1999) *The New Global Economy and Developing Countries: Making Openness Work.*
World Bank. (1997). *Global Economic Prospects and the Developing Countries 1997.*
World Bank. (2000). *Global Economic Prospects and the Developing Countries 2000.*

• The above information is an extract from the World Bank's web site which can be found at www.worldbank.org

Corporate globalisation

Information from Friends of the Earth (FOE)

British banks funding rainforest destruction. Mining corporations digging up World Heritage sites. Big high street brands squeezing out local shops.

All of these social and environmental impacts are the result of corporate globalisation.

What is corporate globalisation?

Did you know?
51 of the world's 100 largest economies are corporations.

Joshua Karliner

The main characteristics of corporate globalisation are:

Bigger and multinational
Companies become larger and operate in more than one country to maximise profit and influence.

Loss of democracy
Economic power is shifting from the general public to the boardrooms.

Social and environmental degradation
Multinationals trade off the policies of one nation against another – resulting in erosion of standards, damage to wildlife and loss of jobs.

Who are multinational companies accountable to?

By law they have to keep their shareholders and investors satisfied.

Investor power
By law, all PLCs have to put maximising profit for their investors first. The big investment houses provide the bulk of the money that business needs to survive.

And it's us – through our pensions, mortgages and even our overdrafts – that the investment houses get their money from.

Investment power houses
Investment houses could choose to make business fairer and greener by only investing in the best companies. Unfortunately because they are silent, the environmental destruction goes on.

Make your money smarter and greener

Did you know?
75% of us want our pension companies to take social and environment concerns into account.

Friends Ivory Sime survey, Aug 2000

We also have the power to make business better
You have the right to know how your money is being used and to speak out if it is not being used in an ethical way. We can challenge big business and win.

Make your money work for you and the environment by challenging the activities of big business.

But this on it's own isn't enough. The economic power of multinationals rivals that of most of the world's governments. This means that there's a serious risk of a loss of public control over corporations.

Government in control?

Companies should be regulated by government. But instead they are using their enormous economic power to extract ever greater privileges from governments.

Did you know?
92% of people believe that multinational companies should meet the highest human health, animal welfare and environment standards wherever they are operating.

MORI poll, 2001

Dirty tricks, filthy companies

Corporations have lobbied national governments hard for:

Handouts
Scotts digs up protected peatlands in the Britain for compost. It wants £40m of UK taxpayers' money to stop.

Rule breaking
Balfour Beatty wanted the UK Government to underwrite the controversial Ilisu Dam in Turkey.

Weakening of standards
Premier benefits from sudden changes in gas exploration rules to enable it to threaten Kirthar National Park in Pakistan.

Corporations and corporate lobby groups also use international agreements and bodies – like the World Trade Organisation (WTO) – to further challenge government power.

Friends of the Earth says:
• Governments should make laws (international and national) to make companies accountable for their actions.

You can use your rights as shareholders and citizens to demand that big business cleans up its act.

• The above information is an extract from Friends of the Earth's web site which can be found at www.foe.co.uk Alternatively, see page 41 for their address details.

Globalisation is good for us

The best way to combat world poverty is to increase trade

By Jack Straw

A banking collapse in south-east Asia causes the closure of a factory in Scotland, the internet allows a doctor in Uganda to receive instant access to expensive medical journals, while the turnovers of such companies as Microsoft and General Motors dwarf the wealth of nations.

These changes generate fear and awe in equal measure. In Genoa, we saw what happens when these spill over into anger. Yet if we want to avoid future summits being held behind barricades, we need to do more to engage those interested in dialogue – and win back people's faith in politics and politicians' ability to make a difference to globalisation.

Attempts to manage change on a global level are in their infancy. But the emergence of a global economy and global society demands that we strengthen global governance.

Critics claim that the multilateral trading system has produced losers as well as winners, especially in Africa, where, south of the Sahara, average income is lower today than it was in 1971. But one of the best ways to reduce poverty in Africa and elsewhere is not to call a halt to globalisation, but to increase trade.

Many serious non-governmental organisations agree. Oxfam recently reaffirmed its support for 'a multilateral rules-based trade system', but pointed out that 'rich countries and powerful corporations have captured a disproportionate share of the benefits of trade'. In this, Oxfam is right. But I would argue that the way to redress these imbalances is to launch a new trade round when the World Trade Organisation meets in Qatar this November. In theory, the conditions are there for every economy to exploit its comparative advantage in the global marketplace.

In practice, poor countries can often compete only in niche markets, especially agricultural ones. The barriers the EU and US have erected to protect agriculture in our own countries effectively block Africa from wider participation in the global economy. If we want to fight global inequality, we should lower these barriers, and allow agriculture to do for Africa what textiles and microchips have done for Asia.

> ### In theory, the conditions are there for every economy to exploit its comparative advantage in the global marketplace

Another criticism levelled at governments is their apparent powerlessness in the face of multinational corporations. The lure of consumer values can distort and reduce the degree to which individuals recognise the power that potentially they have as citizens, and as believers in ideas.

A global market, global brands, worldwide access to each other and to information both give us a sense of strength as consumers, and humble us before the power that has produced this situation. But democratic governments of nation states, acting collectively and internationally, represent the only way in which we can produce an effective balance between the individual as consumer and citizen.

We must do what we can to encourage corporate responsibility. But we cannot leave companies to

regulate themselves globally, any more than we do in our national economies. That requires legislation. The last couple of years have seen joint action to regulate the transport and use of GM crops; to ban the production of harmful agro-chemicals; and to make it a criminal offence for multinationals to corrupt public officials.

There is nothing inevitable about globalisation. It is created and shaped by the choices and decisions of us all. Since the collapse of the Soviet bloc, there is no longer a coherent alternative ideology on offer. The extremists of Genoa have no intellectual alternative beyond a return to isolationism and autarky. Afghanistan and North Korea show that for most of us, this is an unpalatable choice.

And history shows us what happens when these ideas take deeper root. When prosperity in the 1920s took a downturn, most governments responded by protecting their industries behind trade barriers. Some chose the path of totalitarianism. As a result, international trade collapsed and recession became depression, the prelude to war.

Governments face their first great challenge of the post-cold war era. If the global economy stumbles, then we will face a series of difficult choices. We could take the advice of the Stop the World campaigners, retreat into our national economies and close our markets. But this would put at risk the real benefits that globalisation, and global capitalism, have brought to millions. The right choice is to preserve and maximise the benefits while minimising the risks through joint global action; to show our citizens that politics matters and that their democratic choices have a real influence on global forces that are beyond their individual control.

• Jack Straw, Foreign Secretary, will be speaking on globalisation today in Manchester.

Borderless business

Transnationals and the world economy

Giants, heroes, villains

Transnational corporations (TNCs) are the economic giants that roam the earth in search of profit. These huge companies are the main 'players' in the globalisation game, intent on dominating the world economy. They increasingly control trade, investment, finance, technology, communication and culture. But TNCs' image as global employers, big investors and engines of growth is marred by associations with environmental degradation, asset-stripping, workers' rights abuses and corruption throughout the developing world. They can be both villain and hero, but without them globalisation wouldn't exist.

What is a transnational corporation?

The United Nations define a TNC as an association that possesses the means of control of production and services, outside the country in which it was established. Any company with foreign operations is, technically, a transnational. In reality, TNCs are rightly seen as very large, highly sophisticated organisations, richer than many countries and more powerful than many governments.

Transient transnationals

The truly borderless firm is still elusive. TNCs generally use their country of origin as a base to which they return their profits and keep their headquarters. While 10% are based in the South, mainly in Southeast Asia, 90% of TNCs are based in industrialised countries.

What distinguishes the recent period of globalisation is the increasing ease with which big manufacturers can move their operations, and with them the crucial investment that poor countries want. They may stay only a few years before moving on. This means that borders are no real barrier to investment. If a country goes into recession or becomes unstable, as happened in Indonesia

By Steve Tibbett

recently, foreign capital will move with ruthless speed. Labour, on the other hand, is still comparatively immobile. The result is high unemployment, economic disintegration and social unrest.

Power rangers

There are 40,000 transnationals operating around the world. Some of the biggest have larger turnovers than many countries. The largest ten TNCs have a total income greater than the collective income of the world's 100 poorest countries. The Ford Motor Company alone has a turnover bigger than that of South Africa. In 1995 alone TNCs collectively sold $7 trillion worth of products through their foreign affiliates, more, even, than the world's total exports for that year.

Because making a profit is the overarching goal of every TNC their actions may come into conflict with the aims of people and governments. By exercising their enormous power and global reach they can control markets and influence policies. Without regulation TNCs will not deliver the benefits of globalisation to those who need it most.

Governments are further constrained by the insistence of international institutions on 'flexible' labour markets. Unfair trade agreements stifle the leverage of poorer countries. An international reluctance to relieve their foreign debt burden compounds their helplessness. Meanwhile, the transnationals can manipulate markets, pay the necessary bribes and exploit tax loopholes and subsidies. By holding large amounts of different currencies they can even manipulate exchange rates to their advantage. General Electric, for instance, is now the largest financial institution in the US.

The monopoly economy

Transnationals dominate international trade and investment. 500 corporations control 2/3 of all world trade. TNCs are responsible for over 4/5 of all foreign investment. Nearly 1/3 of international trade occurs within individual companies.

Trading is second nature to TNCs. Many foreign operations in the developing world are simply cheap production centres for rich country markets. Some split their operations globally, treating the world as one big assembly line. Others, like the American giant Cargill, have integrated virtually the whole production and market process, from producing raw materials to manufacturing, transportation to finance. By controlling and dominating all these processes, TNCs can trade extremely profitably.

Investment in local companies is another way in which TNCs increase their global reach. With up to 1/4 million affiliated companies world-wide, transnationals can manage their operations at arm's length. Foreign Direct Investment (FDI) is highly sought after by most countries, including the developed ones. At best, it provides jobs, tax revenue and spin-offs for the local economy. At worst FDI is a drain on the domestic economy, with profits repatriated to rich countries, no real technology transfer and local capital reduced to a subsidiary role.

Global employment for a global market

TNCs are large global employers. Between them they employ 73 million people world-wide. In addition, tens of millions are employed in ancillary, sub-contracting and support services to their operations.

But even when sub-contractors are taken into account, transnationals only employ 5-10% of the global workforce. Considering TNCs control 33% of the world's productive assets, they are clearly not the huge boost to employment that might be expected.

Whilst TNCs concentrate in high-tech, 'capital-intensive' industries in the industrialised North, their operations in developing countries tend towards cheaper, 'labour-intensive' production. For many TNCs, cheap, flexible and compliant labour is a good reason, sometimes the only reason, to move South.

Governments keen to attract foreign capital have set up explicitly deregulated areas usually called 'export processing zones' (EPZs). Countries like Mexico, the Philippines, China, Bangladesh and India have seen large increases in employment due to TNC investment in EPZs. But such jobs have largely been low-skill and low-tech and the work is often poorly paid and non-unionised – facts which are advertised in the literature of EPZs as good reasons to invest.

Controlling interests

TNCs are mostly owned by large institutions such as pension funds and insurance companies. That means most of us have a stake in big business and can potentially exert that power and influence over them.

But TNCs are subject to very little real control. National governments are under increasing pressure to deregulate inward investment controls. There is no international regime of regulation specifically designed to control transnationals, yet proposals exist to enable companies to take countries to a special international court if they try to regulate them. Indeed TNCs even have their trading interests backed up by a global judicial and legislative body in the form of the World Trade Organisation. Without regulation of transnationals it is difficult to see how they can be controlled for the good of people and planet.

Increasingly TNCs are setting their own standards for behaviour. Pressure from campaigning organisations like War on Want along with demands from trade unions, consumers and investors, have led some transnationals to produce their own set of rules. These 'codes of conduct' usually cover basic health and safety, child labour, environmental and ethical standards. Most codes do not include union rights as a specific requirement. Companies such as Nike, C&A, Shell and The Gap have all adopted codes, with varying degrees of success.

Other strategies to hold transnationals to account are being implemented on a voluntary basis, but set global standards based on consensus. The UK-based Ethical Trading Initiative brings companies, trade unions and NGOs together to act on global working conditions in a spirit of constructive engagement and the Council on Economic Priorities has set up SA 8000 to audit workplace standards internationally.

Such initiatives do help to keep TNCs in check and help to pave the way for the internationally agreed and enforced regulation that would give real power back to democratic organisations and the people they represent.

YOU can help fight the War on Want
- Joining a trade union means you can give support to international solidarity work and campaigns against worker exploitation around the world. (If you are already a union member push them to do more international work)
- Buying 'fair trade' products gives workers around the world a better deal and allows them a stake in the process of trade
- Joining War on Want means joining the campaign to eliminate the root causes of poverty and oppression

- Supporting War on Want project partners around the world means giving help to organisations who put people before the market
- Joining our 'Invest in Freedom' Campaign means you can use your pension to hold multinationals to account, discouraging exploitation and oppression instead of rewarding it

Globalisation needs regulation. War on Want will continue to press for change. Your support means we can campaign to
- redress the unequal spread of the world's wealth and the unchecked power of multinationals – we should not allow large companies to dictate to people
- reform the institutions of global governance such as the IMF and UN to enable them to regulate transnational corporations
- lobby governments to intervene to ensure that basic rights and conditions are afforded to everybody on the globe
- tax currency speculation to help calm markets and produce revenue for helping to end poverty
- support development schemes such as microfinance, health and education initiatives at local community level where appropriate

With your help we can stand up for workers and against global poverty in all our campaigns. Join us.
- The above information is an extract from War on Want's web site which can be found at www.waronwant.org Alternatively see page 41 for their address details.

© War on Want

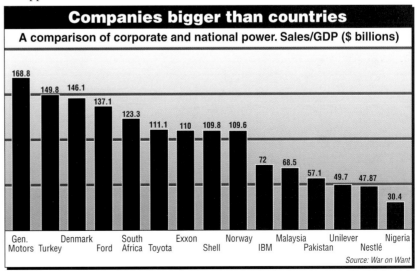

Companies bigger than countries

A comparison of corporate and national power. Sales/GDP ($ billions)

Gen. Motors	168.8	
Turkey	149.8	
Denmark	146.1	
Ford	137.1	
South Africa	123.3	
Toyota	111.1	
Exxon	110	
Shell	109.8	
Norway	109.6	
IBM	72	
Malaysia	68.5	
Pakistan	57.1	
Unilever	49.7	
Nestlé	47.87	
Nigeria	30.4	

Source: War on Want

Globalisation

Making globalisation work for the world's poor

What is globalisation?

This is unlikely to be the first time you have heard about it, and it will not be the last. Even the word itself has different meanings, but overall, globalisation is about processes of change affecting our lives. This information looks at globalisation and encourages you to think about your own points of view on some of the questions it raises.

'Globalisation means the growing interdependence and inter-connectedness of the modern world.'
White Paper on International Development, 2000

This means the way we, a worldwide 'we', rely on each other, and what we do. Where we live has an effect somewhere else.

There are other important aspects of globalisation:

- the principle of 'the market', where the amount of buying and selling is seen as the main measure of companies' success;
- the power of transnational companies, where a third of world trade takes place between trans-nationals or between parts of the same corporation in different countries;
- the internationalisation of culture, where the same goods and services, such as food and television, take over and swallow up local customs and traditions.

The need to manage globalisation

Some people think that globalisation will lead to an increasing gap between the rich and the poor. But globalisation is not an unshapeable force. To others it can be managed to deliver an equitable world and to lift people out of poverty.

'One in five of the world's population – two-thirds of them women – live in abject poverty: on the margins of existence, without adequate food, clean water, sanitation or healthcare, and without education.'
White Paper on International Development, 2000

The UK government has written a White Paper on globalisation. A White Paper is where a government department sets out an agenda explaining its ideas and plans. It also shows any need for new spending or new laws.

The UK government's White Paper makes it clear that globalisation should not be seen as a separate process beyond our control. Instead, globalisation can and should be managed so that it can work for the benefit of the world's poorest people. To make this happen politicians will need to take action to ensure that the gap between the world's rich and the world's poor does not become even wider.

'The central challenge we face today is to ensure that globalisation becomes a positive force for all the world's people, instead of leaving billions of them behind in squalor.'
Kofi Annan, United Nations Secretary General, April 2000

- The above information is an extract from *Global Insights – Making globalisation work for the world's poor* – published by Worldaware for the Department for International Development (DFID). See their web site at www.worldaware.org.uk

© *Worldaware*

Population living below US$1 per day in developing countries 1990 and 1998

	Number of people below US$1 a day (millions)		Poverty rate (%)	
	1990	1998 (est.)	1990	1998 (est.)
East Asia	452.4	278.3	27.6	15.3
Excluding China	92.0	65.1	18.5	11.3
South Asia	495.1	522.0	44.0	40.0
Sub-Saharan Africa	242.3	290.9	47.7	46.3
Latin America	73.8	78.2	16.8	15.6
Middle East/North Africa	5.7	5.5	2.4	1.9
Europe & Central Asia	7.1	24.0	1.6	5.1
Total	1276.4	1198.9	29.0	24.0

Source: World Bank. Global Economic Prospects and the Developing Countries 2000.

Making globalisation work for the world's poor

An introduction to the UK Government's White Paper on International Development

The world is smaller than it has ever been . . . Its six billion citizens are closer to each other than ever before in history.

Each one of us is increasingly connected to people we will never meet, from places we'll never visit. Many of our clothes or shoes will have been made by people thousands of miles away – perhaps those people are laughing at a dubbed version of one of 'our' sitcoms. The fuel in our cars, the microprocessors in our computers, the coffee in our cup – so many of the products we buy in our high street have journeyed half-way around the world. And we're connected in other ways too. For example, jobs in the UK depend on trade with, or investment from, faraway countries. People travel more, but so do pollution and diseases.

Connected world

As the world's population becomes more and more connected the process has been recognised and given a name: globalisation.

And yet, while living standards rise for many as a result of globalisation, more than a billion people on our planet live in extreme poverty, forced to make ends meet on a tiny income and very few basic services. These are the people for whom the shrinking of the planet has delivered no progress.

Eliminating such extreme poverty is the greatest moral challenge the world now faces. In its first White Paper on International Development, published in 1997, the UK Government committed itself firmly to the International Development Targets through which the world's governments have agreed to work to halve extreme poverty by 2015.

But reducing poverty is not just a moral issue. The closer we are connected across the continents, the more we become dependent on each other.

And, if we don't take action now to reduce global inequality, there's a real danger that life for all of us – wherever we live – will become unsustainable.

The UK Government believes that globalisation creates unprecedented new opportunities for sustainable development and poverty reduction. It offers an opportunity for faster progress in achieving the International Development Targets.

But – so far – the benefits of globalisation have been unevenly

---

Reducing poverty is not just a moral issue. The closer we are connected across the continents, the more we become dependent on each other

---

spread – for example while the peoples of East Asia have experienced benefits, millions of people in rural Africa have yet to see any change.

Progress is not inevitable. It depends on political will. And this depends on governments and people across the world.

The challenge is to connect more people from the world's poorest countries with the benefits of the new global economy. And that means globalisation must be managed properly – to benefit everyone.

In publishing its new White Paper on International Development, in December 2000, the Government is setting out an agenda for managing the process of globalisation in a way that works for the world's poor. This article introduces the issues and the Government's key proposals for tackling them.

Good governments work for poor people

It's not enough for people in developing countries to simply say,

---

The International Development Targets

- A reduction by one-half in the proportion of people living in extreme poverty by 2015.
- Universal primary education in all countries by 2015.
- Demonstrated progress towards gender equality and the empowerment of women by eliminating gender disparity in primary and secondary education by 2005.
- A reduction by two-thirds in the mortality rates for infants and children under age 5 and a reduction by three-fourths in maternal mortality – all by 2015.
- Access through the primary healthcare system to reproductive health services for all individuals of appropriate ages as soon as possible, and no later than the year 2015.
- The implementation of national strategies for sustainable development in all countries by 2005, so as to ensure that current trends in the loss of environmental resources are effectively reversed at both global and national levels by 2015.

The UK Government will:
- Work to manage globalisation in the interests of poor people, creating faster progress towards the International Development Targets.

'Yes please, I'd like to take advantage of the benefits of globalisation.' They need governments that listen and that work.

Governments in poorer countries have to create conditions at home that will help the poorest people in their communities find work or a market for their goods that will sustain their families.

While the market fundamentalism of the eighties and early nineties has been discredited, it's now widely accepted that efficient markets are indispensable for effective development.

Developing countries must attract foreign investors. But that's not enough. If the only people who benefit from a new factory or the export of agricultural produce are the rich elite, nothing much has changed.

Policies for people

For globalisation to work for the poorest people, governments must introduce policies that allow companies to conduct their business safely and with a reasonable return. Otherwise they will take their investment elsewhere. So there has to be a stable legal system, where theft is punished, where bribery and corruption are outlawed, where people's human rights are respected and working conditions safeguarded.

Developing countries with effective governments – healthy democracies, with proper management of public finances, effective health and education services, fair law enforcement and a free media –

> *For globalisation to work for the poorest people, governments must introduce policies that allow companies to conduct their business safely*

are far more likely to deliver economic growth for their citizens.

States which invest in basic infrastructure such as water and sanitation, transport, electricity and telecommunications can play a major part in giving poor communities access to global markets.

One of the biggest barriers to development is armed conflict. Its threat to investment, stability and security destroys the conditions for growth. The UK Government will step up international efforts to regulate the trade in small arms. Effective and inclusive states – where all people have a stake in the well-being of the country – are much less likely to suffer the tragic human and economic consequences of violent conflict.

Strengthening the vulnerable

The rights of the poor and their influence on government policy must be strengthened – for example by supporting the groups which are helping the poor speak with a stronger voice: religious organisations are particularly close to the poor; co-operatives, women's organisations, human rights groups,

development NGOs and trade unions could all help.

But globalisation itself can also work here. New information technologies offer news and information from all over the world which can help the poor to be heard. The increased access to information can also be used to bring to a wider audience the plight of a particular people – thus bringing the weight of international public opinion on those who are abusing or exploiting vulnerable people.

The UK Government believes that creating a sound balance between good social policy and good economic policy will provide the surest way to prosperity for developing countries.

The UK Government will:
- Work to promote effective systems of government and efficient markets in developing countries.
- Legislate to give UK courts jurisdiction over UK nationals who engage in bribery overseas.
- Introduce a licensing system to control UK arms brokers and traffickers, and work for tighter controls internationally at the UN conference on small arms.

• The above information is an extract from *Making globalisation work for the world's poor – An introduction to the UK Government's White Paper on International Development* published by the Department for International Development (DFID). See their web site at www.dfid.gov.uk

© Crown Copyright

How to rule the world

Rich nations should stop running the planet and give way to global democracy

T he leaders of the free world present a glowing example to the rest of the planet.

Of the eight men meeting in Genoa this week, one seized the presidency of his country after losing the election.

Another is pursuing a genocidal war in an annexed republic. A third is facing allegations of corruption. A fourth, the summit's host, has been convicted of illegal party financing, bribery and false accounting, while his righthand man is on trial for consorting with the mafia.

Needless to say, the major theme of this week's summit is 'promoting democracy'.

But were the G8 nations governed by angels, they would still be incapable of promoting global democracy. These eight hungry men represent just 13% of the world's population.

They were all elected to pursue domestic imperatives: their global role is simply a by-product of their national mandate. The decisions they make are haphazard and ephemeral.

Last year, for example, the G8 leaders announced that they were determined to achieve the goals of the Kyoto protocol limiting climate change and that they would preserve and strengthen the anti-ballistic-missile treaty.

One man is replaced and all is lost.

Similar problems delegitimise almost every global body. The World Bank and IMF, which apportion votes according to the money they receive, are governed by the countries in which they don't operate.

The five permanent members of the United Nations security council, charged with maintaining world peace, also happen to be the world's five principal arms traders.

The UN general assembly represents governments rather than people: a poor nation of 900m swings, in practice, less weight than a rich nation of 50m.

By George Monbiot

The G8 leaders know that the 'global democracy' they are due to discuss is a sham, and they will do all they can to keep it that way.

There is, we are told by almost everyone, no alternative to the rule of finance and fear.

Writing in the *Guardian* last week, Philippe Legrain, a former World Trade Organisation official, argued that world elections to a world parliament are not realistic. 'Sixty million Britons would not accept 1,300m Chinese outvoting them.'

Mr Legrain has, un-intentionally, presented the anti-globalisation movement with its central challenge.

If those of us in the rich world who are protesting against the inordinate powers of the G8, the World Bank or the WTO are serious about overthrowing unaccountable power, then we must rise to his bait.

In 1937, George Orwell observed that 'every revolutionary opinion draws part of its strength from a secret conviction that nothing can be changed'. Bourgeois socialists, he charged, were prepared to demand the death of capitalism and the destruction of the British empire only because they knew that these things were unlikely to happen.

'For, apart from any other consideration, the high standard of life we enjoy in England depends upon keeping a tight hold on the Empire – in order that England may

live in comparative comfort, a hundred million Indians must live on the verge of starvation – an evil state of affairs, but you acquiesce in it every time you step into a taxi or eat a plate of strawberries and cream.'

The middle-class socialist, he insisted, 'is perfectly ready to accept the products of Empire and to save his soul by sneering at the people who hold the Empire together'.

Since then, empires have waxed and waned, but that basic economic formula holds true: we in the rich world live in comparative comfort only because of the inordinate power our governments wield, and the inordinate wealth which flows from that power.

We acquiesce in this system every time we buy salad from a supermarket (grown with water stolen from Kenyan nomads) or step into a plane to the climate talks in Bonn.

Accepting the need for global democracy means accepting the loss of our own nations' power to ensure that the world is run for our benefit.

Are we ready for this, or is there lurking still some residual fear of the yellow peril, an age-old, long-imprinted urge towards paternalism?

Global democracy is meaningless unless ultimate power resides in a directly elected assembly. This means, of course, that a resident of Kensington would have no greater influence than a resident of Kinshasa.

The Ethiopians would have the same number of representatives as the British (and rather more as their population increases). The people of China would, collectively, be 22 times as powerful as the people of the United Kingdom.

In a truly democratic world, the people's assembly would, unlike the European parliament, be sovereign. All other global bodies would report to it and act on its instructions.

The UN, WTO and other bodies, if they survived at all, would be reduced to the status of the parliament's civil service. But, as the World Citizen Foundation has pointed out, to preserve local democracy its scope must be limited by subsidiarity.

It could not interfere in strictly national decision-making, in other words, but would seek to do only what existing global bodies are attempting – and failing – to do today: resolving disputes, tackling global poverty, defending people from oppression and protecting the world's resources.

But it's not hard to see how a world parliament could bypass and undermine dictatorships. Just as proportional representation in European elections has encouraged us to start questioning our own, flawed system, genuine global democracy would highlight demo-cratic deficits all over the world.

The danger, of course, is that the world parliament might make decisions we don't like very much. We may discover that people living in the world's most populous nations don't want to tackle global warming or to control nuclear weapons. But danger is what democracy is all about.

And it's hard, in truth, to imagine a people's assembly making a worse fist of these issues than the G8 and the warmongers of the security council.

Accepting the need for global democracy means accepting the loss of our own nations' power to ensure that the world is run for our benefit

---

China has curbed its carbon dioxide emissions while energy use in the US has soared. Indeed, the only fair and lasting means of reducing CO_2 (namely 'contraction and convergence', which means working out how much pollution the planet can take, then allocating an equal pollution quota to everyone on Earth) would surely be impossible to implement without a world parliament.

The very existence of a global assembly could help to resolve disputes: people often take up arms only because they have no other means of being heard. I suspect, too, that the World Bank and IMF, whose role is to police the debtors on behalf of the creditor nations, would disappear almost immediately.

A democratic assembly would almost certainly replace them with something like Keynes's 'Inter-national Clearing Union', which would force creditors as well as debtors to eliminate third world debt and improve the balance of trade.

But the democratisation which may or may not result in such changes cannot even be widely discussed until we, the new world order's prosperous dissidents, are prepared to take our arguments to their logical con-clusion, and let go of the power our nations possess and the dis-proportionate wealth which flows from it.

I hope that we, unlike Orwell's bourgeois socialists, are ready for this challenge. If not, we may as well as cancel our tickets to Genoa and stay at home eating strawberries and cream.

Trade

The good, the bad and the decidedly ugly

First things first!
Did you know that international trade is worth four trillion pounds each year? (That's four with twelve zeros after it.) And it just keeps on growing! It is seriously hard to imagine that kind of money but think about everything that is bought and sold around the world, from food to clothes to cars to holidays to toys to computers. Buying and selling all these products, or the raw materials that make them, mounts up to big money.

Most people think it's great that the world can now work together to produce a massive amount of choice in what we can buy at our superstores, But what if the world isn't working together at all? What if the system is working in such a way that the rich keep getting richer and the poor keep

Christian Aid
We believe in life before death

getting poorer? That is exactly what is happening.

International trade is governed by a set of rules. Theses rules control which countries can sell to which other countries, and at what price. Sounds good, rules are definitely needed. Imagine playing football or driving a car if there were no rules – it would result in chaos! But what if the rules are the wrong ones? That would make things a hundred times worse. Football games would become rugby scrums, cars would crash into each other, pedestrians wouldn't

know where to walk, journeys would take a lot longer and people would get hurt. This is exactly what's happening in the world of global trade.

Spotlight on trade rules
Christian Aid thinks there are four main problems with the current trade rules:
1. How they're decided
2. What they do
3. How they're enforced
4. What they don't do.

1. How the rules are decided
International trade rules are made by members of the World Trade Organisation, or the WTO as it's better known. Most countries belong to the WTO and in theory they all have an equal say in how it runs.

But if you're from a very poor country, like Gambia or Malawi, you just can't afford to have lots of people to represent your interests at the WTO headquarters in Geneva, Switzerland. In fact these countries often can't afford to have any at all, while a rich country like Japan pays 25 people to work there all year round.

This means that the richer countries can have all sorts of meetings and make deals between themselves, while the poorer countries don't get a look-in, let alone a say. So it isn't fair from the start.

2. What the rules do

Because the way that trade rules are decided is so unfair, it's no surprise that they hurt poor people rather than help them. But poor countries can't just choose not to trade – they need trade so that they can afford things like health care, education, housing and transport. Here are just a few real-life examples of how the rules don't help poor people.

Farmers in Ghana

Lydia Assosou grows cassava and maize on a small farm near Accra, the capital of Ghana. Like lots of other women in her situation she works incredibly hard to bring up her children and provide for her family. Ghana's government used to help small-scale farmers like Lydia by subsidising the prices of things like seeds, tools and fertiliser.

Ghana's no longer allowed to do this, according to the rules set by international organisations like the World Bank, the International Monetary Fund and the WTO. They're forcing Ghana to liberalise its economy. This means the government has to spend money on making things to sell to other countries, instead of spending money to help farmers like Lydia. The government is also forced to make it easier for other countries and companies to trade in Ghana.

For people like Lydia, this means paying more for seeds, fertiliser and fuel, and earning less from the crops she grows. As if that isn't bad enough, the cuts in government spending also mean the cost of health care, schools and transport has gone up, making it

harder for Lydia to make ends meet.

The Trade for Life campaign believes poor countries shouldn't be forced to adopt rules which make poor people poorer.

HIV drugs in Brazil

Javier is 30 years old. Two years ago his life was turned upside-down when he found out he was HIV-positive. He cut himself off from friends and family because of their reaction, and is fighting a court case to keep his job in the army (which he hopes to win, with the support of GAPA-BA, one of Christian Aid's partner organisations). 'People considered me absolutely incapable, as if from then on I was no longer a human being but something that could be thrown away or something useless.'

Despite all this, Javier considered himself lucky because he had access to the essential anti-retroviral drugs which keep the onset of AIDS at bay. The Brazilian government has worked hard to be able to provide free treatment to people like Javier, by supporting the cheap production of these medicines in Brazil.

But if big US companies get their way, Javier may soon have to face the future without these vital drugs. Under new rules set by the WTO, the USA has threatened to take Brazil to court to stop the production of these cheaper drugs. US companies want to make as much money as they can – regardless of how many people the cheaper drugs

may be keeping alive. If these companies succeed, there's no way that Javier could afford to keep taking the drugs, making his future, and the future of millions of people living with HIV in poorer countries, look decidedly bleak.

'What we all want from countries like the USA is that they put to one side financial interests and instead they and the WTO recognise that our demands are just,' says Javier. 'We are seeking the right to live! And to live well, with quality and respect, even though we carry HIV around within us.'

The Trade for Life campaign believes that rules that allow companies to make profits at the expense of people's lives should be changed.

3. How the rules are enforced

The main way that the WTO enforces its trade rules is by allowing countries to refuse to trade with a country that has broken the rules, but in practice it's completely uneven. Poorer countries like Tanzania know that if they break a trade rule and a richer country like the USA loses out because of it, the USA will impose sanctions. That would be devastating for Tanzania. But if the USA breaks a trade rule and Tanzania loses out, no one in the USA would even notice, let alone mind, if Tanzania imposed sanctions on them! The USA could just go and find another poor country to trade with.

It's far too easy for rich countries to ignore trade rules or get around them, and there's very little that poor countries can do about it.

4. What the rules don't do

Within the WTO there are often no rules when there should be. Some of the biggest companies that trade throughout the world (transnational corporations or TNCs) have far more money and power than individual countries. The US firm General Motors is richer than 37 of the world's poorest countries put together!

For poor people TNCs can be both good and bad. They can provide jobs and new technology, and they can bring money into poor countries. However, because they also want to make as much money as possible, they often underpay workers and abuse the environment. There are no international rules that set standards for how TNCs should work in poor countries; they are free to do what they want. The governments of poor countries are not powerful enough to stop them, so imagine how hard it is for the world's poorest people.

Why get involved?

Well, the United Nations reckon that poor countries are losing out on about £500 billion every year because of current trade rules. Just think what

---

Factories in Sri Lanka

Until recently Pushpa worked in a factory in Sri Lanka that makes clothes for companies like GAP and Nike. The factory is in an area called a Free Trade Zone. This means there are hardly any rules to govern how companies operate. As a result the workers get a really bad deal – low wages, which are often paid late, long hours, unrealistic targets, fines for being one minute late, even limits on how many times they're allowed to go to the loo!

Pushpa wanted to do something about the lack of workers' rights, so she joined a human rights group and became involved in street plays about the unjust treatment of workers in the factories. A manager from her factory happened to see Pushpa in a play and soon after things got really difficult. First they gave her unreasonably high targets – and in factories like these, not reaching targets means getting paid less. Then she kept getting moved to different parts of the factory so that she was never able to get quick enough at a task to reach her target. She was made to do jobs which would normally be done by machine – not only did this take much longer, so again she couldn't reach her target, she also ended up with cuts all over her hands.

The company that owns the factory was trying to get rid of Pushpa because she spoke out against conditions there. In the end it worked and Pushpa resigned. You might think that's a good thing given that the job was so awful, but no job means no income and most women like Pushpa can't afford not to work. Because all the factories in the area work in much the same way, Pushpa's left with few choices and no rights.

The Trade for Life campaign believes that there should be trade rules for how companies behave, as well as governments.

---

that could buy! Christian Aid has worked out that this is enough money to clear the world of landmines, save the sight of 30 million people in poor countries and rid the world of the disease tuberculosis (TB) for ever.

We believe that everyone has the right to life in all its fullness. As you can see, many people do not have that. If there is *anything* we can do to change the injustice of the current situation we should do it. And there is so much we can do.

• The above information is an extract from Christian Aid's youth pack *Trade for Life*. Visit their web site at www.christian-aid.org.uk or see page 41 for their address details.

© *Christian Aid*

Globalisation and trade

Information from Global Eye

The ways in which goods and information are moved between countries are becoming easier. Information technology is driving these improvements by enabling companies to move money and ideas instantly at the click of a mouse. Consequently, people are becoming more interconnected and interdependent, a trend known as 'globalisation'. Although globalisation can be felt in different ways, this article will look at its effects on *trade* between countries as we move towards a more rapid, open trading system.

The World Trade Organisation: breaking down trade barriers

International trade has been going on for centuries, but the removal of trade barriers that countries use to protect their businesses, such as tariffs and quotas on imports, is likely to quicken the pace of globalisation. This way, countries are encouraged to produce the goods and services that they can make more cheaply than their competitors; in other words, 'do what you do best and trade for the rest'. To ensure fair play in this more open trade system, the World Trade

Organisation (WTO) was set up in 1995. The WTO can impose penalties on countries that break the rules. However, critics argue that many poor countries do not have enough representatives at the WTO. Consequently WTO representatives of richer countries are able to influence the rules so that trade barriers in the developed world, such as the EU's Common Agricultural Policy, continue to protect their businesses and give them an advantage. Nevertheless, there are moves to reform the WTO so that every country can benefit from the process of globalisation.

Transnational companies . . . friend or foe?

Although trade rules are agreed between countries, it is companies that do the trading. Many believe that the real winners of a more open trade system will be the large companies that already dominate world trade. By setting up factories in different countries to manufacture or assemble components, companies can produce goods more cheaply and efficiently. Today, these 'transnational' companies (TNCs) control two-thirds of world trade. With more open trade, TNCs have greater freedom to shift location to developing countries where wages are lower and they are less restricted by environmental controls.

Competition between poorer countries to attract foreign investment is fierce. To offer the best deal to TNCs, wages are sometimes forced down so low that human rights groups have found working conditions in some factories that they describe as modern-day slavery. Also, jobs may involve merely fixing together imported parts and materials, which do little to build local skills and expertise.

However, TNCs can help developing countries by creating jobs and generating investment that can be used to educate local people to develop homegrown skills and expertise. Local businesses benefit too as factory workers spend their earnings. South Korea is a country that has gained from these knock-on effects. By manufacturing goods cheaply, many Koreans now enjoy a standard of living similar to Europeans thanks to the profits from exports. China is now following suit. Fuelled by foreign investment, China is now the world's biggest exporter of clothes, toys, shoes and electronic goods, and average incomes in urban areas are ten times greater than they were 20 years ago.

Different trading opportunities

Selling goods and services in a more open world market should bring more money into a country, but it depends what you are selling, and whether you have the resources, infrastructure and technology to take advantage of the new market conditions. Today, the poorest 10% of the world's population take part in less than 0.5% of the world's trade.[1] Many lack the technology, infrastructure and manufacturing base to compete with companies in the developed world. Instead, people rely on the sale of primary commodities even though their world price compared to manufactured goods, or 'terms of trade', is now at its lowest for 150 years. To afford the same amount of manufactured imports, poorer countries may have to produce more primary commodities, which could use up scarce land and resources in some countries. On the other hand, many African and South American countries do have abundant natural resources that could be traded. This could help people escape poverty in the future.

Making globalisation work for the poor

The processes of globalisation are certainly complicated. Whilst they bring new opportunities, they also present some tough challenges ahead. With a more open market place, poor communities in many countries could escape poverty as they gain access to new markets to sell their goods and services. It could be easier to obtain technology that could help poor communities develop in sustainable ways.

Poorer countries will need to invest in roads, ports and airports so people in remote areas can benefit as well. Many poorer countries that do not have enough money of their own will need investment from abroad. To attract foreign investment, governments need peaceful conditions and to prevent corruption. Poorer countries need to be fully involved in any changes in world trade and to avoid the possible drawbacks of globalisation. By managing globalisation in this way, it could help bring lasting benefits to the fifth of the world's population that currently live in extreme poverty.

Source
1 Christian Aid 2000

• The above information is an extract from *Global Eye*, www.globaleye.org.uk (Summer 2001 edition). *Global Eye* is the magazine about world development published by Worldaware. See page 41 for their address details.

What's wrong with world trade?

Information from Friends of the Earth (FOE)

What is trade?

Trade affects almost everything we do. Put simply, it's the everyday activity of buying and selling goods and services – something we're all involved in. It doesn't even have to involve money. If you babysit for your neighbours in return for a box of home-grown vegetables from their garden, that's trade.

However, in today's global economy, trade is thought of in rather a different way. The volume of goods and services we buy from abroad has increased dramatically and we have come to associate trade with financial transactions, international commerce and long-distance transport.

In the past, governments sometimes controlled trade through military force. More recently, they have ensured that imports and exports have been controlled through trade restrictions such as taxes, quotas and bans. Despite seemingly different approaches, the aim has usually been the same – protecting the domestic economy.

Now, however, economists argue that protecting the domestic economy, often known as protectionism, blocks international trade and is uneconomic, inefficient and eventually leads to job losses. This argument has prevailed allowing free trade or trade liberalisation to become widely accepted worldwide. Over the past 50 years many governments have opened up their markets to foreign trade and investment, so now goods and services move between countries more freely than ever before – annual global trade topped US$7 billion in 1998.

Trade liberalisation and the World Trade Organisation (WTO)

Supporters of trade liberalisation believe that countries adopting free trade can improve their economic

Friends of the Earth

prospects. To do this they must specialise in producing what they are best at and then trade with each other. To do this they must open their markets, by dropping any trade restrictions and forcing their companies to compete internationally.

The idea is that this increases competition and efficiency, which in turn drives down prices, making products more attractive to consumers and increasing demand. Business booms, national income increases and everyone benefits as the wealth trickles down. However, there is a great deal of evidence suggesting that the reality of free trade is rather different (see next section).

Friends of the Earth believes that this is because the overall costs to society outweigh any benefits. What has occurred is freer not fairer trade. Economic growth continues to benefit the already rich while the decisions of the WTO work to overturn the laws of elected governments, damage communities and scar the environment. The main winners

---

In 1960, the 20 per cent of the world's population living in the richest countries were 30 times richer than the poorest 20 per cent: by 1997, they were 74 times richer

---

from trade liberalisation are rich countries, large companies and the already wealthy. The main losers are poor people and countries, small businesses and workers. Those that benefit strongly support further liberalisation, yet many millions more are implacably opposed to it for a variety of reasons.

Trade is governed by a set of rules overseen by the World Trade Organisation (WTO). The WTO also oversees the trade liberalisation process, with its 130-plus member governments participating in negotiating rounds in which they agree to open their markets step-by-step so long as others do the same. The WTO is probably best known for handling controversial trade disputes between member states and it is this, its ability to authorise hefty trade sanctions, that gives it its clout.

A number of governments had planned to use the WTO's meeting in Seattle, in November 1999, to launch a new round of trade liberalisation or market-opening negotiations. If this had happened, WTO rules could have been greatly extended to cover many new areas, including foreign investment and government procurement. However, because of disagreements between governments on several issues – and because of unprecedented public opposition – the Seattle negotiations collapsed. Nevertheless some governments, led by the European Union, continue to push for a new round.

Who's protesting against the global economy?

The protest against the World Trade Organisation's activities at Seattle was the biggest protest in the US since the anti-Vietnam war demonstrations. Around 50,000 people protested, most peacefully. Seattle was a remarkable political landmark because it demonstrated that people from all walks of life, from all over the world, were sufficiently concerned about the impacts of trade liberalisation to work together to oppose a new round. Nearly 1,500 organisations from 89 countries around the world, including Friends of the Earth, signed an international statement rejecting a new round and calling for a review of current trade rules and agreements.

But what brought about this unprecedented level of opposition? Five reasons are outlined below.

The gap between the rich and poor is getting wider

Shockingly, 1.3 billion people are still obliged to survive on less than one dollar a day and consumption in Africa is now 20 per cent lower than it was in 1980. Basic needs – such as adequate nutrition and literacy – are still not being achieved. Furthermore, between 1975 and 1997, as global trade expanded, the average wealth per person in the world's 31 richest countries increased, yet in 31 (mostly poor) countries it actually declined. In 1960, the 20 per cent of the world's population living in the richest countries were 30 times richer than the poorest 20 per cent: by 1997, they were 74 times richer. A link between globalisation and increasing inequality is already acknowledged by the United Nations.

More production and trade has led to the excessive use of natural resources

Trade liberalisation encourages richer countries to consume more and poorer countries to export more, often destroying irreplaceable natural resources. Over-fishing now means that 60 per cent of the world's ocean fisheries are at or near the point at which yields decline. A huge area – 56 million hectares – of forest was lost globally between 1990 and 1995. And at the rate we are using resources such as petrochemicals and metals, the resulting climate change, health impacts of pollution and habitat damage are already exceeding sustainable levels – and growing as consumption rates increase. If UK consumption levels and patterns were to be matched globally, we would need eight planets to provide the resources needed.

Companies are becoming so powerful it's difficult to control their activities

The world's largest companies have access to high-level decision-makers on trade issues, because governments assume that what's good for business is good for everyone else. Yet these companies are looking to strengthen their position in a competitive global economy by increasing their own access to foreign markets and reducing standards and costs (to please shareholders). They are the driving force behind government moves to open up markets.

However, because of the pressures of international competition, many companies – particularly in the oil, banking and retailing sectors – are taking steps to reduce costs through mergers and re-organisations. About two-thirds of world trade is now accounted for by just 500 companies – and some of these make more money than many countries. In 1997, the five largest companies in the world together had sales that were greater than the combined incomes of the world's 46 poorest countries. This makes it increasingly difficult for any government to resist their demands and take other concerns on board.

Small businesses and farms can't compete and jobs are being lost

Smaller businesses and farms simply can't compete with the influence and market power of these new global giants, with implications for consumer choice. Mergers have also led to a large number of people losing their jobs. In addition, businesses are increasingly able to shift their offices and factories to countries with cheaper labour and fewer anti-pollution laws. In fact, the pressure of global competition is causing many countries to adopt more 'flexible' but weaker labour policies in order to cut their labour costs (France, Germany, Egypt, Argentina and Chile have all done this). Overall, job insecurity is on the increase worldwide.

Poorer countries have to negotiate on unequal terms

The WTO is heavily influenced by a small group of very powerful trading nations or blocs – including the US, the EU, Canada and Japan. Other nations risk being isolated in the global economy if they do not join the WTO. However, as many poorer countries discovered at Seattle, they were often excluded from meetings where important decisions were due to be taken.

What's wrong with trade liberalisation?

The overall impact of trade on people worldwide and the environment can clearly be seen if we look at oil, the world's most widely traded commodity (by value).

Since 1988, more than 100,000 new oil exploration wells have been drilled. In the process, an area the same size as the US and Europe combined has been awarded to companies searching for oil. This threatens many indigenous peoples – including the U'wa in Colombia, the Karen in Burma, and the Baka and Efe indigenous peoples in the Congo basin – along with untouched forest in 22 countries and coral reefs in 38 countries.

Oil, together with products derived from it, such as petrol, is one of the world's most versatile resources. Countries' economies are based on oil, which is used to generate energy. Many industries, such as those that manufacture plastic products, are also dependent on oil as a raw material. International trade requires oil for transport fuel in ships, planes and lorries. It comes as no surprise that demand for oil increased by 30 per cent between 1985 and 1998 and is projected to increase by a further 15 per cent by 2010.

Yet oil can seriously damage our environment and communities. Oil exploration often destroys valuable habitats such as forests and wetlands and its movement often results in oil spills. The use and disposal of oil and oil products causes pollution, including carbon dioxide, an important climate-changing gas. In fact, pollution from land, discharges from ships and illegal dumping account for the 2.5 million tonnes of oil released into the oceans every year. These impacts are made worse by escalating car use.

Nevertheless, some countries that produce and export oil have not benefited from trade liberalisation. This is partly because the liberalisation of the oil trade during the 1980s and 1990s produced a glut of oil on the market, forcing its price down (but also stimulating car use). On average, people in some of the poorer major oil-producing countries – such as Venezuela, Mexico, Gabon and Nigeria – witnessed a fall in their wealth.

Oil companies are now some of the most powerful institutions in the world. The recent merger between Exxon and Mobil created a company with annual sales in excess of US$190 billion making it more powerful – in economic terms – than Hong Kong or Turkey. The production, trade and marketing of petroleum products remains the lifeblood of the company and it has not sought to invest in other more environmentally friendly kinds of energy (such as wind or solar). Consequently, the company is opposing any efforts to agree an international climate change treaty.

Exxon-Mobil is not the only company that has strengthened its position in the oil industry. Mergers have also occurred between BP and Amoco and between Total and Petrofina. Projected job losses from the Exxon-Mobil merger were put at 9,000 people; the BP-Amoco partnership was expected to cost 7,000 jobs.

As with other products, the solution to these global impacts may not be directly related to trade – for example, we all need to consume less. However, the trade liberalisation process has made it more difficult for governments to restrain production and consumption and maintain key health and environmental standards.

What does Friends of the Earth want?

Friends of the Earth is not anti-trade. What Friends of the Earth wants is fairer trade – trade that is conducted more sustainably, with the benefits shared more equally. In particular, we want to see the importance of local communities and economies around the world acknowledged, supported and strengthened. Trade within borders is at least, if not more important than trade across borders.

How can this be achieved?

Friends of the Earth believes that we need to stop the trade liberalisation process, rollback the power and authority of the WTO and review the trade system and its rules to assess what has or has not been achieved – economically, environmentally and socially. In particular, there should be no new round of trade negotiations.

There are a number of first steps that should be taken to restrain the WTO. In particular:

- WTO rules must not apply to sectors critical to human or animal welfare or the environment. Trade rules should not be permitted to cover food and water, basic social services or health and safety.
- The remit – and hence the power – of the WTO should not be expanded to include new issues such as biotechnology.
- WTO rules should not override laws designed to protect local communities and the environment.
- The WTO should not be permitted to oversee disputes with non-trade impacts, for example on people or their environment, internally. Disputes should be held in an independent court.
- The WTO should be more democratic and transparent: and it should reflect the needs of all, including people that have been largely excluded from the global economy (including poor countries and people, women, children, workers and indigenous peoples).

In addition, there need to be strong and binding rules governing the activities of corporations. Governments should also be allowed to screen and set standards for incoming investors.

What can you do?

There are three key ways to help encourage fairer trade. You can keep yourself well informed by backing organisations which are working on trade issues, like Friends of the Earth. You can make wise lifestyle choices and you can be an active citizen. Here's how:

Keep informed

Visit the Friends of the Earth Europe web site for up-to-date campaign information: www.foeeurope.org/trade/about.htm

Make wise lifestyle choices

It's important that people living in rich countries – who consume most of the world's resources – reduce the impact of our lifestyles. Consumers in Europe can:

- Buy locally produced (preferably organic) produce where possible.
- Ask shops and supermarkets to stock locally produced (and organic) products and a full range of fair trade products. And ask stores to adopt policies to develop fairer trade.
- Buy environmentally friendly products and the increasing number of fair trade products that are now on the market – chocolate, breakfast cereals, coffee, tea, honey and other preserves, rice and pasta to name just a few.
- Increase efforts to reduce, reuse or recycle.

Be an active citizen

- Write to your Head of State demanding that the rules of the WTO should not be extended and that a full, independent assessment of the trade system is conducted. Demand the right for products to be labelled so that consumers can make an informed choice as to the kind of product they buy (e.g., organic, sustainably harvested or fair trade).
- Ask your Government to assist in the development of markets for fair trade products.

Contact details:
Friends of the Earth, 26-28 Underwood St., LONDON, N1 7JQ. Tel: 020 7490 1555, Fax: 020 7490 0881. E-mail: info@foe.co.uk Web site: www.foe.co.uk

© Friends of the Earth

Trade

Information from CAFOD

What is trade?

Trade is – buying and selling. When you buy a CD or a pair of trainers you are taking part in trade. You exchange money for goods or services.

Countries, companies, workers and consumers take part in trade. Workers make the goods e.g. clothes, or grow the crops e.g. pineapples. Companies pay the workers and sell the goods or crops. Other companies might also be involved in a more indirect way e.g. in advertising, transport, or market research.

Trade can involve more than one country – a shirt might be sewn in Mexico, have the buttons put on in the United States, then be sold in France.

Countries try to attract companies to set up business (invest) because this brings jobs, and earns foreign currency. Countries and companies import and export goods and services. People who buy the goods are called consumers.

Who sells what? – global trade

Third world countries used to sell mainly raw materials (e.g. fruit, cotton, copper). Today they also sell manufactured goods; especially those that need a lot of workers to make (labour intensive). Third world countries have an advantage over rich countries because wages are lower – it costs less to make a pair of shoes in a poor country than in a rich country.

Raw materials

Good – you don't need complex technology and you can earn money selling raw materials abroad.

Problems for the Third World

- The price of raw materials

> ### Fact file
>
> - From 1980-1997 world trade in goods tripled from £1 trillion to over £3 trillion
> - From 1960-1990 the poorest 20 per cent of the world's people saw their share of world trade fall from four per cent to one per cent
> - When you buy a pair of trainers that costs £44 only £1.71 goes to the workers in Asia who made them

changes a lot and often. This makes it hard to plan

- Prices for raw materials are often very low. You have to sell a lot of pineapples to be able to afford a computer
- It is difficult for third world countries to start making hi-tech goods like cars. They do not have the technology. Rich countries sometimes try to stop them – they don't want the competition in case they lose out

Manufactured goods

Good – industry often brings jobs. If you have a job you earn money to live on.

Problems for the Third World

- Companies move from country to country looking for the cheapest work force
- Countries and companies are under a lot of pressure to compete – to make the best product at the cheapest prices. This can mean cutting corners on health and safety, paying low wages, and working long hours

Trade – free or fair?

When countries import goods they charge a special tax called a tariff. In

recent years the trend in world trade has been to reduce tariffs.

Some countries have signed free trade agreements with each other – this means that they promise to reduce tariffs on goods from countries which have signed up to the agreement. For example, Mexico has a free trade agreement with the United States and Canada (NAFTA) that began in 1994.

The World Trade Organisation (WTO) is the biggest organisation promoting tariff reductions on global trade.

Free trade

Good – low tariffs should mean cheaper goods and more trade

Problems for the Third World

When trade rules are agreed, rich countries try to make sure they benefit e.g. tariffs will be removed from US maize sold in Mexico. US maize is cheaper than Mexican maize – farmers in Mexico could go out of business. E.g. the US government has used the WTO to stop Europe giving preference to Caribbean bananas. Caribbean economies will suffer because they depend heavily on banana exports.

Fair trade

Fair trade guarantees higher, more stable prices for third world producers. CAFOD supports the Fairtrade Foundation, which works with third world producers. Look out for these fairly traded products:
* Cafédirect
* Clipper tea
* Divine chocolate

Ethical trade

Large supermarkets, clothes and shoe shops buy more and more of their goods from the Third World. Consumers are worried by stories they hear about the low wages paid to workers, and the bad working conditions. Some companies have introduced 'codes of conduct' for their suppliers – these set out minimum standards on wages and working conditions.

The Ethical Trading Initiative (ETI) brings together companies, aid agencies like CAFOD, and trade unions to try to develop effective

---

Fact file
* TNCs account for two-thirds of world trade.
* Of the world's 100 largest economic entities 51 are TNCs and 49 are countries. Shell's sales are the same size as the economy of South Africa.

---

ways of introducing codes of conduct so that workers really benefit. Members of the ETI include:
* Sainsbury
* Tesco
* Marks and Spencer

Who sells what? – Transnational corporations (TNCs)

TNCs are international companies. They may have their headquarters in Hong Kong but their factories in Wales or China. You would recognise the brand names that they own, but might not know the name of the TNC.

Fact file

TNC – Unilever
Brands include – Blue Band, Flora, I can't believe it's not butter, Brooke Bond, PG Tips, Red Label, Chicken Tonight, Oxo, Bird's Eye, Cornetto, Feast, Magnum, Solero

TNC – Nestlé
Brands include – Nescafé, Crosse & Blackwell, Findus, Perrier, Aero, KitKat, Rolo, Smarties, Quality Street

---

What's the problem?

It is hard for governments to control TNCs because a TNC can move business and factories around the world. Governments need to attract TNCs to create jobs, but they may have to offer incentives like lower tax bills, or build special roads or transport systems. The Multilateral Agreement on Investment (MAI) could make it even more difficult to control TNCs. Visit WDM's website for more information.

Additional information
Useful websites
www.wdm.org.uk
Information from the World Development Movement (WDM) about TNCs, and the proposed Multilateral Agreement on Investment (MAI)

www.eti.org.uk
Ethical Trading Initiative

www.wto.org
World Trade Organisation

www.fairtrade.org.uk
Fairtrade Foundation

Useful reports
(available from libraries or try UN websites)
UNCTAD Trade and Development Report 1998
World Investment Report 1998
UNDP Human Development Report 1999

For more information about the work of CAFOD or to arrange a development day or in-service training, contact the Schools Section schools@cafod.org.uk

• The above information is an extract from CAFOD's web site which can be found at www.cafod.org.uk
© CAFOD

Eight broken promises

Why the World Trade Organisation (WTO) isn't working for the world's poor

Hypocrisy and double standards characterise the behaviour of industrialised countries towards poorer countries in world trade. This article identifies eight broken promises made by the rich to the poor. At the forthcoming World Trade Organisation summit in Doha, the biggest global meeting on trade since Seattle, WTO members must end the cycle of broken promises and build the foundations of a more equitable world trading system.

Summary

This article identifies eight broken promises made by rich countries. Each one has cost developing countries the opportunity to gain a fairer share of global wealth. Each one has denied people in developing countries the chance to escape poverty.

If rich countries honoured their promises to developing countries to deliver improved market access and fairer treatment at the World Trade Organisation (WTO), globalisation would be producing real benefits for poverty reduction.

Unfortunately, Northern governments have failed to act on their commitments. They are maintaining trade policies that skew the benefits of world trade away from poor countries and towards the rich, reinforcing already obscene levels of global inequality in the process.

If industrialised countries are serious about making trade work for the poor, and about restoring the credibility of the WTO, they need to arrive at the forthcoming WTO ministeral conference in Doha – with a clear timetable for converting their encouraging words into real action.

Since the end of the Uruguay Round of world trade talks in 1994, promises have been in steady supply. Rich countries have pledged to phase out protection against imports of textiles and garments, to scale down agricultural subsidies, and to remove trade barriers against the poorest

Oxfam

countries. They have made commitments to ensure that WTO rules on intellectual property and investment do not undermine development prospects. And they have promised technical assistance to enhance the capacity of developing countries to participate in the WTO and in trade.

So many promises – and such little action. The record of industrialised countries in the area of trade policy is one of heroic under-achievement. They have collectively reneged on every commitment made. Among the headlines:

- Developing countries are losing around US$100bn a year through unfair protectionist policies, according to the United Nations.
- Tariff barriers in rich countries are four times higher for poor countries than for industrialised countries.
- Northern governments have increased agricultural subsidies, instead of cutting them, to US$350bn a year. Barriers to agricultural trade cost developing countries US$20bn a year.
- Rich countries have failed to fulfil their commitment to phase out Multi-Fibre Agreement restric-

---

The debate over whether globalisation is inherently good or bad for the poor is not a helpful starting point for addressing one of the key challenges facing the international community

---

tions on textile and garments exports – one of the developing world's most important manufactured exports.

- The world's poorest countries – the Least Developed Countries – face some of the highest tariff barriers on their exports.
- Intellectual property and investment rules are being applied in a manner that undermines social and economic welfare in poor countries and further marginalises them.
- International trade is one of the motors of globalisation. As a source of economic growth, it has never been more important to global prosperity. Wealth generation through trade is running at an all-time high. Yet as governments prepare for the WTO Ministerial Conference in Doha, the credibility of the multilateral trading system is running at an all-time low. The system is facing a crisis of legitimacy. That crisis is the product not of anti-globalisation protest, but of the blatant hypocrisy and double standards that govern the behaviour of rich countries towards poor countries.
- The current debate over whether globalisation is inherently good or bad for the poor is not a helpful starting point for addressing one of the key challenges facing the international community. International trade has the potential to act as a powerful source of economic growth and poverty reduction. Yet that potential is being lost. The reason: rich-country governments are refusing to extend to poor countries the market opportunities they need. Instead, they are reinforcing a system that leaves countries representing four-fifths of the world's population with less than one-fifth of world exports.
- Access to industrialised country markets is not a panacea for

poverty reduction; national governments must promote equitable access to assets such as land, credit, and education to achieve an equitable distribution of the benefits of trade among communities within countries. Yet by failing to fulfil their promises, industrialised countries undermine efforts by developing countries to use trade as a means of promoting poverty reduction.

- As the threat of a prolonged global recession increases and protectionist pressures in industrialised countries mount, there is a real threat of further marginalisation. We all stand to prosper from a more equitable and stable global trading system. And we all stand to lose from trade

policies that deny some of the world's poorest countries a fair share of the wealth generated by globalisation.

• The above information is an extract from Oxfam's web site which can be found at www.oxfam.org.uk

Alternatively see page 41 for their address details.

© *Eight broken promises: Why the WTO isn't working for the World's Poor? An Oxfam Briefing Paper, reproduced with permission of Oxfam Publishing, 274 Banbury Road, Oxford, OX2 7DZ*

Mind the gap

Globalisation doesn't work for everyone. Millions of people are being sucked deeper into poverty because of decisions made by big organisations in countries far away

Eleven-year-old Liberia lives in Arua in north-western Uganda. She may not know it, but two organisations called the World Bank and the International Monetary Fund (IMF) have a huge impact on whether she and millions of other children and young people go school.

'I'm supposed to go back to school next term with 1,000 shillings, but I don't think I'll be able to pay the fees. I'll still go to school, and maybe they'll send me home'.

Many of the world's poorest countries, including Uganda, owe the World Bank and the IMF huge sums of money. Although their leaders aren't elected, these organisations are powerful enough to pressurise governments into making decisions that ignore their people's real needs.

Going to school is one of the best ways to escape poverty, but Liberia may not be able to because her government has been told to introduce school fees so it can repay more debt. Many other countries with big debts have been also been forced to start charging for

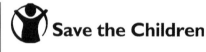

essentials like education and healthcare.

Global rules like these, made by officials in rich countries who are mainly interested in money, often ignore the most fundamental needs of the world's poorest people. If the rules don't change, the gap between rich and poor could turn into an abyss.

Many of the world's poorest countries, including Uganda, owe the World Bank and the IMF huge sums of money

---

In the 1970s, high oil prices enabled banks in richer countries to give huge loans to countries needing

to develop, often after centuries of colonisation. When oil prices fell, loan interest rates increased, making them impossible to pay back. More loans were given on the condition of introducing structural adjustment policies, which aimed to improve the economy. Instead of helping, the loans often made things worse. In the 1990s, organisations including Save the Children began to publicise the negative impact of debt, and by the end of 2000, 22 countries had started receiving some debt relief. However, the majority are still spending more on loan repayments than on health and education.

The campaign continues – find out more at www.dropthedebt.org or call 020 7922 1111.

• The above information is an extract from *RightAngle*, the magazine produced by Save the Children. For more information see their web site at www.savethechildren.org.uk or see page 41 for their postal address details.

© *Save the Children*

Poverty in an age of globalisation

Information from the World Bank

Hopes and fears in an integrating world

The past century has seen more advances in global prosperity, and more people lifted out of poverty, than in all of human history. There are many reasons for this achievement, but globalisation has played an important catalytic role. Yet, paradoxically, there is a widespread perception that globalisation is having a detrimental impact on the poor.

In spite of the wide usage and the intensive debate that is now under way, there is no precise or widely-accepted definition of globalisation. Globalisation can be summarised as the global circulation of goods, services and capital, but also of information, ideas and people. It has shaped all of the 20th century, albeit with large cyclical variations, and has become an increasingly visible force in recent decades. Although there are many factors that have spurred and in turn have been reinforced by globalisation, two have played a particularly important role in contributing to its accelerating pace in the 1980s and 1990s. The first is technical progress especially in information technology, international communication and global transportation. Not only goods but also services and knowledge can flow much more easily because of innovations such as the Internet. The second major development is the shift in policy orientation as governments everywhere have reduced barriers that had curbed the development of domestic markets and their links to the international economy.

These forces of integration have contributed to global prosperity and development transformation. Despite a population increase from 1.8 billion to 6.0 billion, and despite giant political upheavals and wars, real average income per person has at least quintupled over the past century. Average global per capita income today exceeds that of the richest country at the turn of the century. And today's average life expectancy exceeds that of the lead country 100 years ago.

The pace of progress has also accelerated. It took the United Kingdom some 60 years to double income per capita in the 19th century. Today we have seen that countries with populations ranging from millions to a billion can double income per head in a decade (China, Japan, Korea) and quickly reach life expectancy of more than 70 years. By enabling and indeed 'pressuring' countries to adopt best practice pioneered elsewhere in the world, globalisation has been an important agent for change and transformation.

Yet there are sharply divided views on the benefits that it has brought developing countries and the poor. One view is that globalisation has 'left out' most developing

> *There is no precise or widely-accepted definition of globalisation*

countries because they have been unable to reap its benefits. Another, contrasting view (often advanced together with the former observation) is that there has been 'too much' globalisation and that this has been detrimental to the poor.

Facets of globalisation

The evidence suggests that developing countries are becoming more integrated with the global economy and that the pace has accelerated over the past decade. But except for the successful East Asian economies, the level and pace of their integration has until recently lagged behind that of the developed countries. Moreover, progress on integration has been uneven between developing countries, in trade and international finance and more recently in terms of information technology.

Trade

There has been a growing divergence over the last three decades in shares of trade, between those countries actively participating in the global economy and those that do not. For many of the poorest, Least Developed Countries (LDCs) the problem is not that they are being impoverished by globalisation, but that they are in danger of being largely excluded from

it. The minuscule 0.4 per cent share of these countries in world trade in 1997 was down by half from 1980.

Financial flows

Similarly, although financial flows to developing countries have also grown dramatically, they remain concentrated: fifteen emerging market countries, mainly in East Asia, Latin America and Europe, accounted for 83 per cent of all net long-term private capital flows to developing countries in 1997. Sub-Saharan Africa as a whole received only 2 per cent of the total.

Information technology

Rapid technological change and global connectivity has generated an information and knowledge gap between countries, the so-called 'digital divide'. About half of the world's population has never made a phone call, while Africa has only 2 per cent of the world's telephone mainlines. Only 2.4 per cent of the world population are users of the internet, almost all of whom are concentrated in the OECD countries. Roughly 90 per cent of internet host computers are located in high-income countries that account for only 16 per cent of world population. Overcoming this digital divide is going to be a key challenge for developing countries in the coming years.

Globalisation and poverty

Poverty trends

It is important to distinguish between the incidence of poverty as a percentage of a total population and the absolute number of the poor. The share of the population in poverty has declined for developing countries as a whole (from 28.3% in 1987 to 24% in 1998 based on $1/day and from 61% in 1987 to 56% in 1998 based on $2/day) and in all developing regions except Sub-Saharan Africa and Eastern Europe and Central Asia. Declines have been pronounced and sustained over a longer time period for the most populous developing countries. For example, the incidence of poverty in India measured by the official poverty line fell from 57% in 1973 to around 35% in 1998, whereas the incidence of poverty fell from 60% to 20%

Only 2.4 per cent of the world population are users of the internet, almost all of whom are concentrated in the OECD countries

---

between 1985 and 1998 for Indonesia. Standards of living have also improved. Infant mortality rates globally have been cut in half during 1970-1997, from 107 to 56 per thousand; and life expectancy has risen from 55 years to 67 years. However, in spite of this broad-based progress, more than 40 developing countries with 400 million people have had negative or close to zero per capita income growth over the past thirty years. And the absolute number of poor has continued to increase in all regions except East Asia and the Middle East. Overall, despite impressive growth performance in many large developing countries, absolute poverty worldwide is still increasing.

Globalisation, growth and poverty

Globalisation has played an important catalytic role in reducing poverty in developing countries through its impact on growth. More open economies, and those who have been more successful in accelerating their pace of integration, have recorded the best growth performance, whereas developing countries with inward-oriented policies have suffered from poor growth rates. A recent study estimates that an increase in the ratio of trade to GDP by one per cent raises the level of income by one-half to two per cent (Frankel and Romer, 1999). By stimulating higher growth, integration can have a strong positive impact on poverty reduction. There is now robust cross-country empirical evidence that growth is on average associated one-for-one with higher incomes of the poor. There are, however, significant variations in this relation between countries. In the aggregate, no more than 50% of the variation in the poverty measure is explained by differences in growth. Another way to state this is to say

that poverty is affected by many factors other than growth. For example, initial levels of income inequality and changes in inequality may also impact poverty. There seems to be, therefore, large scope for designing more pro-poor growth policies although more research is needed to deepen our understanding of the poverty impact of specific policies. Also, average changes in poverty mask a great deal of churning associated with growth and structural change, in which some lose and others gain.

Direct impact of trade integration on the poor

Trade integration can also affect the poor beyond and above its impact through higher growth, but these effects are not clear cut. In general, for the poorest countries, opening up trade will expand the production of goods intensive in the use of low-skilled labour, but the demand for the least-skilled labour may not be boosted by trade and may be adversely affected by technological change spread by globalisation. For middle-income countries, the impact on the poor is likely to be even less clear cut based on the prevalence of the poor in previously sheltered sectors relative to potentially expanding sectors, and the competition coming from large low-income countries. The impact of trade liberalisation will also vary depending on the post-liberalisation pattern of inequality, which in turn will depend on the way trade reform is managed and on other accompanying reforms. There is evidence, however, from a large developing country sample of medium-to-long-term growth episodes that, on average, in economies/periods of fast trade integration, income growth of the poor has kept pace with mean income growth (*Global Economic Prospects 2001*, forthcoming). By contrast, in economies/periods of slow or declining outward orientation, on average the poor have tended to fall behind.

• The above information is an extract from *Poverty in an Age of Globalisation* published by the World Bank. See page 41 for their contact details.

© 2001 The World Bank Group

Poverty

Information from CAFOD

What is poverty?

'Not having the minimum income level to get the necessities of life.'
Concise Oxford Dictionary

'More than a lack of what is necessary for material well-being, poverty can also mean the denial of opportunities and choices most basic to human development – to lead a long, healthy, creative life; to have a decent standard of living.'
The State of Human Development 1998

4.4. billion people live in developing countries. Of these:
- three-fifths lack basic sanitation
- almost one-third have no access to clean water
- a quarter do not have adequate housing
- a fifth have no access to modern health services
- a fifth of children do not attend to the end of primary school
- a fifth do not have adequate protein and energy from their food supplies

'Everyone has the right to a standard of living – adequate for the health and well-being of him/herself and his/ her family, including food, clothing, housing and medical care and necessary social services . . . Everyone has the right to education.'
Universal Declaration of Human Rights.

Mind the gap

In 1997 the richest fifth of the world's population had 74 times the income of the poorest fifth.

The top three billionaires have assets greater than the combined GNP of all least developed countries and their 600 million people.
Human Development Report 1999

Things can only get better

Over 80 countries have lower incomes per person.

Measuring poverty

According to internationally accepted standards anyone earning less than 60p a day (US $1) is living below the poverty line, i.e., does not earn enough to live on.

Percentage of people living below the poverty line

Europe and Central Asia	3.5%
Latin America and the Caribbean	23.5%
Sub-Saharan Africa	38.5%
Middle East and North Africa	4.1%
South Asia	43.1%

There are three major ways of measuring a country's wealth:
- Gross National Product (GNP) is the annual total value of all goods produced and services provided in a country
- Gross Domestic Product (GDP) is the same, excluding deals with other countries

- Human Poverty Index (HPI) does not use money as the only factor. It includes education, length of life and living standards
(For more information see *Human Development Reports* since 1997)

GNP per person 1997

United Kingdom	£12, 648
Uganda	£200
Ethiopia	£67

Causes of third world poverty

Trade
Third world countries lose out through unfair trade agreements, lack of technology and investment, and rapidly changing prices for their goods.

Work and globalisation
Better communications and transport have led to a 'globalised' economy.

Companies look for low-cost countries to invest in. This can mean that, though there are jobs, they are low-paid.

OKAY, OKAY – WE'LL BUY THE BOWL...

Debt

Third world countries have to pay interest on their debts. This means they cannot afford to spend enough on basic services like health and education; nor on things like transport or communications that might attract investment.

Land

If you have land you can grow your own food. But many people in the Third World have had their land taken over by large businesses, often to grow crops for export.

War or conflict

When a country is at war (including civil war) basic services like education are disrupted. People leave their homes as refugees. Crops are destroyed.

Health

Affordable or free health care is necessary for development. In poor countries the percentage of children who die under the age of five is much higher than in rich countries. HIV/AIDS is having a devastating effect on the Third World.

> 'HIV is now the single greatest threat to future economic development in Africa. AIDS kills adults in the prime of their working and parenting lives, decimates the work force, fractures and impoverishes families, orphans millions . . .'
>
> Callisto Madavo,
> vice-president of the World
> Bank, Africa region 1999.

Food and education

Affordable, secure food supplies are vital. Malnutrition causes severe health problems, and can also affect education. Without education it is difficult to escape from poverty. This becomes a vicious circle; people who live in poverty cannot afford to send their children to school.

Gender

When we measure poverty we find differences between the level experienced by men or boys, and women or girls. Women may be disadvantaged through lack of access to education; in some countries they are not allowed to own or inherit

land; they are less well paid than men.

Environment

A child born in an industrialised country will add more to pollution over his or her lifetime than 30-50 children born in the Third World. However, the third world child is likely to experience the consequences of pollution in a much more devastating way. For example, annual carbon dioxide emissions have quadrupled in the last 50 years. This contributes to global warming, leading to devastating changes in weather patterns. Bangladesh could lose up to 17% of its land area as water levels rise.

Human Development Report 1998

Tackling poverty

2015 poverty targets
Members of the Organisation for Co-operation and Development (OECD) agreed these after the 1995 Copenhagen summit. They aim to reduce poverty in third world countries by at least one-half by 2015.

20/20 initiative
At the same summit some governments agreed that 20% of aid and 20% of the budget of the developing country receiving that aid would be spent on basic services.

Aid
Access to basic services for everyone would cost approximately US$40 billion more per year than is spent now. This is 0.1% of world income.

World military spending is US$780 billion per year. US$50 billion is spent on cigarettes in Europe every year.

Fair trade

Fair trade guarantees higher, more stable prices for third world producers. Look out for products with a Fairtrade Mark.

Debt campaigning

Find out more about Cafod's campaign on the web site.

Environment

Look out for local Agenda 21 activities. The next UN environment summit will take place in 2002.

Useful web sites

www.eti.org.uk
Ethical Trading Initiative

www.wto.org
World Trade Organisation

www.fairtrade.org.uk
Fairtrade Foundation

www.undp.org
United Nations Development Programme

www.oneworld.org
Non-governmental organisations links site

www.worldbank.org
World Bank, includes statistics and reports

www.oecd/dac
OECD information on aid and development

www.grid.unep.ch/geo
UN site on environment issues

For more information about the work of CAFOD or to arrange a development day or in-service training, contact the Schools Section at schools@cafod.org.uk

• The above information is an extract from CAFOD's web site which can be found at www.cafod.org.uk Alternatively, see page 41 for their address details.

© CAFOD

Tackling global poverty

Brown calls for $50bn global poverty fund

Gordon Brown will call on the world's wealthiest countries today to establish a $50 billion fund to tackle global poverty as a part of a 'new deal' for the world economy.

In a speech to the New York Federal Reserve, he will call for 'a campaign against poverty and for social justice'.

His proposal is based on a report for the United Nations by Ernesto Zedillo, a former president of Mexico, which tried to identify how much money would be needed to meet internationally agreed targets on poverty.

These call for world poverty to be halved by 2015, infant mortality to be reduced by two-thirds, and for all children to have access to primary education.

The Zedillo report concluded that meeting the targets by 2015 would require an increase in the international aid budget of $50 billion – £35 billion – a year. Mr Brown will propose it be called the '2015 Fund'.

Treasury officials said it was too early to put a figure on how much Britain might eventually contribute.

By Benedict Brogan,
Political Correspondent

Britain gives 0.31 per cent of its national wealth to overseas aid, compared to an average of 0.22 per cent in other industrialised nations.

However, Mr Brown will say that he is prepared to examine proposals for raising the cash, including the Tobin Tax on transactions in financial markets. But he will warn against confusing the need to raise extra cash for overseas development with the means by which the money is raised.

'The issue is whether we manage globalisation well or badly, fairly or unfairly'

Speaking ahead of this weekend's World Bank and International Monetary Fund meeting in Ottawa, Mr Brown will outline a plan to encourage trade and economic development in poorer countries.

He will tell fellow finance ministers that they must band together to close the 'funding gap' facing the Third World by offering extra development aid in exchange for commitments to reduce corruption.

No country committed to economic development and poverty reduction should be denied the chance to make progress because of the lack of investment.

Following this week's trade talks in Qatar, the Chancellor will also defend economic globalisation from the criticisms made by those who believe free trade favours big business at the expense of poorer countries.

'Some people will say the issue is whether we have globalisation or not,' he will say. 'In fact, the issue is whether we manage globalisation well or badly, fairly or unfairly.

'Managed badly, globalisation will leave whole economies and millions of people in the developing world marginalised. Managed well, globalisation can and will lift millions out of poverty and manage the high road to a just and inclusive global economy. So the question is not whether we move forward with globalisation, but how.'

Is there any alternative to globalisation?

Information from the Globalisation Guide

Anti-globalisation

What if the tide could be rolled back? What would those who oppose globalisation want to see? There is a wide range of opponents to globalisation, some of whom have quite different visions, ranging from Marxist revolution to less defined objectives, such as the 'end to poverty'.

However, there is a current of opponents who favour devolution of power from the global to the local. This view is well expressed in an alternative framework by the US based International Forum on Globalisation (www.ifg.org/beyondwto.html). Local government and institutions should be strengthened and global institutions weakened. Whatever can be done at a local level should be.

The mandate and powers of the WTO should be significantly reduced in accordance with the following observation of Indian scholar/activist Vandana Shiva: 'The future is possible for humans and other species only if the principles of competition, organised greed, commodification of all life, monocultures, monopolies, and centralised global corporate control of our daily lives enshrined in the WTO are replaced by principles of protection of people and nature, the obligation of giving and sharing diversity, decentralisation and self-organisation enshrined in our diverse cultures and national constitutions.'

Global trade and investment rules should be subordinated to national and local governments' decisions about conditions on investment within their borders. Every government has the right to set development priorities, protect the commons, set performance requirements on investment, control financial speculation and curb capital flight.

Global trade rules should be subordinate to global environmental agencies and agriculture should be eliminated from global trade rules to allow countries to pursue food security and sustainable farm policy.

There should be a fund created to alleviate poverty with revenue raised through a tax on currency transactions, along with other forms of global taxation.

Links

- A prolific writer on life after capitalism is David Korten, who argues for a rediscovery of communities that are self-organising and cooperative. http://iisd.ca/pcdf/
- There has been a series of 'declarations' by non-government organisations and political groups opposed to globalisation, outlining some elements of their alternate visions.
'WTO – Shrink or Sink!' The Turn Around Agenda is a declaration sponsored by the Ralph Nader affiliated Public Citizen. www.citizen.org/pctrade/gattwto/ShrinkSink/shrinksink.htm
- A declaration by a group of non-government organisations outlined some principles for an alternative to globalisation at the 2000 United Nations General Assembly entitled *NGO Vision for an Alternative Framework* www.wtowatch.org/library/admin/uploadedfiles/NGO_Vision_for_an_Alternative_Framework.htm

- The Asia Europe Dialogue on Alternate Political Strategies produced a declaration, entitled, *Paving The Way To A New World: Let Us Globalise The Struggle.* www.ased.org/resources/appeals/global/bangkok.htm

Pro globalisation

Supporters of globalisation argue that it can be rolled back and point to the period between the first and second world wars as evidence. The increase in world trade as a proportion of world GDP was proportionately greater between 1870 and 1914 than it has been since 1975. That expansion was stopped, not just by the first world war, but by the loss of support for free trade which followed. Tariffs and controls on capital were imposed around the developed world. This led directly to the 1930 depression and indirectly to the second world war.

There is clear danger in the gathering strength of opposition to globalisation that it could be halted again. The consequences of a decline in world trade would immediately be felt with rising unemployment throughout the trading world. The poorest countries of the world would also be affected by a fall in aid and opportunities for trade.

A weakening of the institutions of the global order, such as the WTO, would leave them unequal to the task of adjudicating between nations. The fate of the League of Nations at the end of the 1930s provides a parallel example of the cost of weak international institutions.

It is not clear what alternate form of economic production to the corporation the opponents of globalisation have in mind. However, the sharing of risk in the limited liability corporation has proven a robust framework for the development of innovation, wealth and the advance in global living standards.

Although trade and economic integration could be undone by concerted political opposition, it is not possible to turn back the globalising influence of communications technology.

Links

- A speech by the British Trade minister, Stephen Byers, spells out the consequences of reversing globalisation. www.dti.gov.uk/ministers/speeches/byers040800.html
- In a speech delivered in 2000, the director general of the World Trade Organisation, Mike Moore, considers the consequences of a backlash against liberalism. www.wto.org/english/news_e/spmm_e/spmm39_e.htm

• The above information is an extract from *The Globalisation Guide* web site which can be found at www.globalisationguide.org

© *Australian APEC Study Centre*

ADDITIONAL RESOURCES

You might like to contact the following organisations for further information. Due to the increasing cost of postage, many organisations cannot respond to enquiries unless they receive a stamped, addressed envelope.

CAFOD – The Catholic Agency for Overseas Development
Romero Close
Stockwell Road
London, SW9 9TY
Tel: 020 7733 7900
Fax: 020 7274 9630
hqcafod@cafod.org.uk
Web site: www.cafod.org.uk
CAFOD is the development agency of the Catholic Church in England and Wales and works in partnership to tackle the causes of poverty regardless of race, religion or politics.

Christian Aid
35 Lower Marsh
Waterloo
London, SE1 7RT
Tel: 020 7620 4444
Fax: 020 7620 0719
E-mail: info@christian-aid.org
Web site: www.christian-aid.org.uk
Christian Aid works in over 60 countries helping people, regardless of religion or race, to improve their own lives and tackle the causes of poverty and injustice.

Corporate Watch
16b Cherwell Street
Oxford, OX4 1BG
Tel: 01865 791391
E-mail: info@corporatewatch.org
Web site: www.corporatewatch.org
Corporate Watch's approach is to investigate corporate structures and the system that supports them more broadly, rather than solely criticising the individual companies for bad behaviour. We are committed to ending the ecological and social destruction wrought by the corporate profit motive.

Friends of the Earth (FOE)
26-28 Underwood Street
London, N1 7JQ
Tel: 020 7490 1555
Fax: 020 7490 0881
E-mail: info@foe.co.uk
Web site: www.foe.co.uk
As an independent environmental group, Friends of the Earth publishes a comprehensive range of leaflets, books and in-depth briefings and reports.

Oxfam
Oxfam House
274 Banbury Road
Oxford, OX2 7DZ
Tel: 01865 311311
Fax: 01865 312600
E-mail: oxfam@oxfam.org.uk
Web site: www.oxfam.org.uk
Oxfam GB is a development, relief, and campaigning organisation dedicated to finding lasting solutions to poverty and suffering around the world.

Save the Children
17 Grove Lane
Camberwell
London, SE5 8RD
Tel: 020 7703 5400
Fax: 020 7703 2278
Web site:
www.savethechildren.org.uk
www.savethechildren.org.uk/rightonline
www.savethechildren.org.uk/education
Save the Children is the leading UK charity working to create a better world for children. We work in 70 countries helping children in the world's most impoverished communities. We are part of the International Save the Children Alliance, which aims to be a truly international movement for children. Produces a wide range of materials. Ask for their catalogue.

War on Want
Fenner Brockway House
37-39 Great Guildford Street
London, SE1 0ES
Tel: 020 7620 1111
Fax: 020 7261 9291
E-mail: mailroom@waronwant.org
Web site: www.waronwant.org
Campaigns against world poverty, working in partnership and solidarity with people across the globe. Provides material aid to empower, educate and energise initiatives which confront the causes rather than the symptoms of poverty and injustice.

Worldaware
Echo House
Ullswater Crescent
Coulsdon
Surrey, CR5 2HR
Tel: 020 8763 2555
Fax: 020 8763 2888
E-mail: info@worldaware.org.uk
Web site: www.worldaware.org.uk
and www.globaleye.org.uk
Worldaware is UK-based and works to raise awareness of international development issues. For over thirty years, Worldaware has been a driving force behind the incorporation of development education resources into the school curriculum. Produces the publication *Global Eye* and web site www.globaleye.org.uk

The World Bank
1818 H Street, N.W.
Washington, D.C. 20433
USA
Tel: + 1 202 477 1234
Fax: + 1 202 477 6391
Web site: www.worldbank.org
The World Bank Group is one of the world's largest sources of development assistance. In Fiscal Year 2001, the institution provided more than US$17 billion in loans to its client countries. It works in more than 100 developing economies with the primary focus of helping the poorest people and the poorest countries.

INDEX

agriculture
    and global trade rules 40
    and globalisation 1-2
    subsidies 33
AIDS/HIV
    in the developing world 38
    HIV drugs in Brazil 25
anti-globalisation protests 7, 12, 13, 17
    and trade liberalisation 28-9
anti-globalisation views 2, 7, 12-13, 39-40
arms sales, control of 22

Berlin Wall, fall of the 3
Brazil, HIV drugs in 25

capital market flows, and globalisation 14, 15
capitalism
    defining 3
    expansion of 3
    and the World Bank 5
children, and globalisation 1-2, 34
China
    economic reforms 15
    and global democracy 24
Cold War, end of the 3
competition, and the World Trade Organisation 11
consumption
    increase in rates of 29
    lifestyle choices and fairer trade 30
corporate globalisation
    criticisms of 8-10, 16
    and global trade 9-10
    and trade liberalisation 29
    and the World Trade Organisation 11

debt
    defining 4
    developing countries 34, 37
deforestation, and trade liberalisation 29
democracy
    and corporate globalisation 16
    global 23-4
    and the Internet 1
    and the World Trade Organisation 11-12
developing countries
    aid to 4, 38
    financial flows to 36
    and globalisation 1-2, 12-13, 14-15, 35-6
        British public opinion on 7
        making it work 20, 21-2, 27
    and international trade 31-2, 33-4, 35-6
        unfair protectionist policies 33
    and structural adjustment policies 2, 10, 34
    and transnational companies 27
    and the World Trade Organisation 29, 33-4

economic change, and globalisation 1-2
economic growth, poverty and globalisation 36

education
    in developing countries, and poverty 34, 38
    international development targets 21
employment
    'flexible' labour policies and trade liberalisation 29
    and globalisation 21, 37
    and TNCs (Transnational Corporations) 18-19
environmental agencies, global 40
environmental awareness, and corporate globalisation 16
environmental effects
    of globalisation 7, 11
    of oil production 29-30
    of trade liberalisation 29
ethical trade 4, 32
Ethical Trading Initiative (ETI) 2, 19, 32
European Union (EU)
    Common Agricultural Policy 26
    and free trade 13
    and the Quad 4

fair trade 4
    products 30, 32, 38
    ways to encourage fairer trade 30
farms, and trade liberalisation 29
food production, fair trade products 30
free trade
    and the anti-globalisation movement 12-13
    defining 3-4
    and developing countries 32
    loss of support for 40
    see also trade liberalisation

G8 nations, and global democracy 23, 24
GATT (General Agreement on Tariffs and Trade),
    Uruguay Round 15, 33
GDP (Gross Domestic Product) 37
    and world trade 40
Ghana, international trade and farmers in 25
global democracy 23-4
global trade *see* international trade
globalisation
    alternatives to 39-40
    anti-globalisation views 2, 7, 12-13, 39-40
    and children 1-2, 34
    debate on 7-40
    defining 2-3, 14, 20, 35
    origins of 3
    supporters of 40
    see also corporate globalisation; developing countries
GNP (Gross National Product) 37
Government policies
    on free trade 13
    White Paper on International Development 20, 21-2
health care
    international development targets 21
    in poor countries 38
HPI (Human Poverty Index) 37

ACKNOWLEDGEMENTS

The publisher is grateful for permission to reproduce the following material.

While every care has been taken to trace and acknowledge copyright, the publisher tenders its apology for any accidental infringement or where copyright has proved untraceable. The publisher would be pleased to come to a suitable arrangement in any such case with the rightful owner.

Overview

Globalisation, © Save the Children, *What is globalisation . . .*, © Australian APEC Study Centre, *A global glossary for beginners*, © Save the Children, *The World Bank*, © Guardian Newspapers Limited 2001, *The IMF*, © Guardian Newspapers Limited 2001.

Chapter One: The Debate

Britain turning against globalisation, © MORI, *What's wrong with corporations?*, © Corporate Watch, *Corporate globalisation*, © Corp Watch, *World poverty, 1820-1998*, © Bourguignon and Morrison (2001), Chen and Ravallion (2001), © *Dump those prejudices*, © Guardian Newspapers Limited 2001, *Bridging the global divide*, © Guardian Newspapers Limited 2001, *Assessing globalisation*, © 2001 The World Bank, *Corporate globalisation*, © Friends of the Earth, *Globalisation is good for us*, © Guardian Newspapers Limited 2001, *Borderless business*, © War on Want, *Companies bigger than countries*, © War on Want, *Globalisation*, © Worldaware, *Population living below US$1 per day in developing countries 1990 and 1998*, © The World Bank, *Making globalisation work for the world's poor*, © Crown Copyright is reproduced with the permission of the Controller of Her Majesty's Stationery Office, *How to rule the world*, © Guardian Newspapers Limited 2001, *Trade*, © Christian Aid, *Globalisation and trade*, © Worldaware, *What's wrong with world trade?*, © Friends of the Earth, *Trade*, © CAFOD, *Eight broken promises*, © Oxfam, *Mind the gap*, © Save the Children, *Poverty in an age of globalisation*, © The World Bank, Poverty, © CAFOD, *Tackling global poverty*, © Telegraph Group Limited, London 2001, *Is there any alternative to globalisation?*, © Australian APEC Study Centre.

Photographs and illustrations:

Pages 1, 25, 32 :Pumpkin House, pages 4, 8, 14, 27, 34, 37: Simon Kneebone, pages 6, 22, 31: Bev Aisbett, pages 13, 35, 40: Fiona Katauskas.

Craig Donnellan
Cambridge
April, 2002